Dictionary *of* Idioms & Phrases

Published by
Lotus Press Publishers & Distributors

Dictionary of Idioms & Phrases

Shabnam Gupta

Lotus Press
4735/22, Prakash Deep Building,
Ansari Road, Daryaganj,
New Delhi - 110002

Lotus Press : Publishers & Distributors
Unit No. 220, 2nd Floor, 4735/22, Prakash Deep Building,
Ansari Road, Darya Ganj, New Delhi- 110002
Ph.: 98118-38000
• E-mail : lotuspress1984@gmail.com
www.lotuspress.co.in

Dictionary of Idioms & Phrases

ISBN: 978-81-8382-255-8

Printed & Published by : **Lotus Press Publisher & Distributors,** New Delhi-02

To

Booty and Sanam
The light of my life....

PREFACE

Idioms are a happy and carefree bunch of words put together to express a specific meaning. They can convey this meaning only when they are together, else the gist is lost. This is because they do not follow rules of grammar or syntax, and do not lend themselves readily to any logic, explanation or reasoning. So while I am '*In* the loop' I could be '*Out* of sorts' or '*At* a loss.'

Idioms are unique and do not like to be translated. Even if you try, you cannot translate 'Apple of my eye' or 'In apple-pie order' or 'donkey's years' exactly. One can study the English language and still not be familiar with the meaning of idioms. To understand the full import of idioms, one has to know the culture, the history and the time period during which it was coined.

Idioms are particular about their buddies, and so sometimes the preposition following the word can change its meaning altogether – for example, 'get over', 'get over with', and 'get over it' convey totally different meanings.

So, get a grip on yourself since this book is up for grabs.......

—Author

CONTENTS

A

Aback

Taken aback: taken by surprise.

Usage– Harish was *taken aback* by the boy's aggressive retaliation.

ABC

Elementary knowledge.

Usage– The younger crop of politicians does not know the *ABC* of politics.

Abide by

Follow.

Usage– Yusuf was asked to *abide by* the rules of the academy.

A bird in hand is worth two in the bush

It is better to have small but real benefit, rather than a greater but imagined one.

Usage– Anwar wanted to wait for the IIT admission list, but thinking that *a bird in hand is worth two in the bush,* he decided to pay the fees in the other college instead.

Able bodied

Strong, robust.

Usage– The regime wanted all *able bodied* persons to enlist in the army.

About turn

Change direction or stand.

Usage– The leader of the opposition did an *about turn* and joined the ruling party.

Above board

Honorably open, frank and fair.

Usage– The business dealings of the big company were *above board*.

Above one's station

Beyond one's position.

Usage– She married well *above her station*.

Above one's means

To spend more than one's income.

Usage– It is foolish of Manish to live *above his means*.

Absolute power corrupts absolutely

Too much power can go to one's head.

Usage– Jatin did not want his son to join politics because he knew that the young boy would not be able to handle the position of power, since *absolute power corrupts absolutely*.

A bunch of fives

A fist made by five fingers together.

Usage– The youth made *a bunch of fives* to scare the little boy.

Absent minded

Inattentive, remiss, lacking concentration.

Usage– Anant is an *absentminded* professor.

Actions speak louder than words

What one practices is more important than what one preaches.

Usage– Amar gives alms to beggars regularly in front of his children, because after all, *actions speak louder than words.*

Ace in the hole

Secret trump card.

Usage– The businessman used his existing factory as an *ace in the hole* to clinch the contract.

A chain is only as strong as its weakest link

Literal

Usage– When our school team could not score the crucial goal, our coach realized that *a chain is only as strong as its weakest link.*

Acid test

A test giving sure and confirmed results.

Usage– Getting selected in the IIM was the *acid test* of Manohar's intelligence.

Across the board

Without exception

Usage– The legislation was passed *across the board.*

Act of god

Beyond human control.

Usage– The devastating earthquake was unfortunate, but an unforeseen *act of God.*

Account for

Explain, clarify, give details.

Usage– The drunk driver will have to *account for* his negligence.

A diamond in the rough

Someone who is goodhearted but lacks social finesse.

Usage– Usman loves his rustic cousin even though he is *a diamond in the rough.*

Add fuel to fire

Incite, to worsen matters.

Usage– The politician's speech was intended to *add fuel to fire.*

Add insult to injury

Make matters worse after hurting someone.

Usage– The teacher *added insult to injury* by making the least scoring student stand in a corner.

Addle brained/ headed

Scatterbrain, empty, muddled, confused.

Usage– Most of the models I came across were *addle headed* girls without any focus or direction.

Ad verbum

Verbatim, Word for word.

Usage– Lata memorized the speech *ad verbum.*

A fate worse than death

A misfortune which makes life unlivable.

Usage– The prisoners of war had suffered *a fate worse than death* in the enemy camp.

A feather in one's cap

An honor or achievement.

Usage– When Rahul won the Businessman of the Year award, it was yet another *feather in his cap.*

A fool's paradise

An imaginary world.

Usage– When the writer's manuscript was rejected for the fifth time, he realized that he had been living in *fool's paradise.*

After one's own heart

Well liked, respected, admired.

Usage– My friend is *after my own heart* when it comes to sightseeing.

After someone's blood

Seek revenge.

Usage– The dreaded gangster was *after Shilpa's blood* after she testified against him.

A friend in need is a friend indeed

The true test of a good friend is in tough times.

Usage– When Maya's mother was undergoing chemo-therapy, her friend was by her side. After all, *a friend in need is a friend indeed.*

Ages

For a long time.

Usage– My brother has not written to me for *ages* now.

Agree to disagree

Accept contradictory viewpoint with grace.

Usage– The ad hoc committee formed to examine the cost of living in the country *agreed to disagree* with the previous survey's data and facts.

A house divided against itself cannot stand

Rifts within the family lead to downfall.

Usage– Ravana was defeated because his own brother Vibhishan turned against him. Just goes to prove that a *house divided against itself cannot stand.*

Air of absurdity

An appearance of foolishness.

Usage– Her brother is such a clown, he generally has an *air of absurdity* about him.

A legend in one's own lifetime

A living person of considerable fame.

Usage– Amartya Sen, the Nobel Prize winner, economist and philosopher is *a legend in his own lifetime.*

A little bird told me

Undisclosed source of information.

Usage– The famous gossip magazine starts every piece of story thus: *a little bird told me.*

A little knowledge is a dangerous thing

Incomplete information is harmful.

Usage– She didn't want to question the doctor too much about his prescription, fearing he might think that *a little knowledge is a dangerous thing*

Alive and kicking

In good health.

Usage– Dhiraj's grand-father has proved all doctors wrong, and is *alive and kicking* at the ripe old age of 90.

All at once

Suddenly.

Usage– *All at once,* there was pin drop silence in the hall.

All and sundry

Everyone included.

Usage– The law of our country applies to *all and sundry.*

All of a sudden

Suddenly; without warning.

Usage– The cricketer's mood changed *all of a sudden,* and he refused to answer any other question.

All over the place

Everywhere.

Usage– Mohan's toys were *all over the place.*

All the glitters is not gold

All that looks good may actually be worthless.

Usage– The recent stability in the economy has not generated as many jobs; obviously *all that glitters is not gold.*

All is fair in love and war

Unusual circumstances justify unusual means.

Usage– Shruti married her sister's exhusband; guess *all is fair in love and war.*

All there

Completely sane; fully alert.

Usage– Granny may be old, but she's *all there;* you can't call her senile.

All thumbs

Awkward and clumsy.

Usage– Akriti is *all thumbs* when it comes to knitting and stitching.

All the same

Nevertheless.

Usage– The boys tried to save the pup, *all the same* he died.

All the way

From beginning to end.

Usage– When Sanjhri's mother was under going treatment for cancer, her friend was with her *all the way.*

Allow for

To take into consideration.

Usage– My Math teacher tries to *allow for* correct working of the sums as much as she does for the correct answer.

A man after my own heart

Someone you like.

Usage– Hira is also an passionate about environmental issues; he is *a man after my own heart.*

All along

All the time.

Usage– *All along* my sister said she wanted to go for a trip, but at the last minute she is backing out.

Along with

In the company of.

Usage– Next time when I go camping, I shall take my friend *along with* me.

A nation of shopkeepers

The English

Usage – Hemal told his English buyer that it was difficult to understand his lax business dealings considering that he came from *a nation of shopkeepers*.

An eye for an eye, a tooth for a tooth

Taking revenge.

Usage– The constable shot down two fellow policemen after they raped his daughter; he wanted *an eye for an eye and a tooth for a tooth.*

Answer the call of nature

To defecate.

Usage– The driver stopped the car to one side of the road to *answer the call of nature.*

Any and every

Everyone.

Usage– This machine needs a skilled operator, cannot be run by *any and everyone.*

A place for everything and everything in its place

Tidy and specified place.

Usage– Mother wanted me to clean up my room. Remember, she said, *a place for everything and everything in its place.*

Apple of the eye

Someone very dear.

Usage– Mashud is the *apple of his mother's eye.*

Apple pie order

In perfect order.

Usage– Masaba's mother likes to keep her house in *applepie order.*

Apply for

Usage– Hamsa has *applied for* a visa to the US.

Apply oneself to

To dedicate to.

Usage– Father asked Ranjan *to apply himself* to studies more seriously.

Argue one out of

To convince by reasoning against.

Usage– It is difficult to *argue someone out of* his prejudices.

A riddle wrapped up in an enigma

A mystery or puzzle.

Usage– The reclusive actress prided herself on being *a riddle wrapped up in an enigma.*

A rose by any other name would smell just as sweet

The name doesn't change the intrinsic nature.

Usage– When her best friend called her names, her mother kissed her and said, '*A rose by any other name would smell just as sweet.*'

Around the clock

All day and night.

Usage– The department store is open *around the clock.*

Arm in arm

Holding each other's arms.

Usage– I saw the two little boys walking *arm in arm.*

Arms race

Competition among nations in building weapons.

Usage– The *arms race* between the Superpowers has brought us to the brink of another war.

A safe pair of hands

Someone solid and dependable.

Usage– Romesh wanted *a safe pair of hands* to handle his carpentry work.

As good as one's word

Keeping one's word.

Usage– When Paresh promised that he would take my car for servicing, he was *as good as his word.*

As alike as two peas in a pod

Identical or similar.

Usage– The actress and her sister are *as alike as two peas in a pod*.

As brown as a berry

Brown in colour.

Usage– Hamid's new pup was *as brown as a berry.*

As busy as a bee

Occupied, busy.

Usage– Meira's mother manages the factory and her house; of course she is always *busy as a bee.*

As cool as a cucumber

Calm and unruffled.

Usage– Farida is *as cool as a cucumber* when it comes to crisis handling.

As dead as a dodo/doornail

Deceased and lifeless.

Usage– The goose lying in the grass was *as dead as a dodo.*

As fine as frog's hair

Extremely fine and delicate.

Usage– Madhurima wanted a painting brush which had bristles *as fine as frog's hair.*

As fit as a butcher's dog

Fit and healthy.

Usage– The beggar's son looked *as fit as a butcher's dog.*

As good as gold

Well behaved and sincere.

Usage– Bambi's old car is still *as good as gold.*

As it were

So to speak.

Usage– He is an aristocrat and a nobleman, a man of eminence *as it were,* and someone you looked up to.

As luck would have it

By chance, coincidence.

Usage– Shruti wanted to go to college, but *as luck would have it* she did not get through.

As old as the hills

Quite old.

Usage– The dilapidated log cabin looked *as old as the hills.*

As pleased as punch

Very happy.

Usage– When little Evan was praised for being brave, he looked *as pleased as punch.*

As snug as a bug in a rug

Very comfortable.

Usage – The new student felt *as snug as a bug in a rug* in his hostel in no time at all.

As white as snow

Very fair.

Usage– Sonam's skin is *as white as snow.*

Ashes to ashes dust to dust

From the Bible: 'Dust thou art, and unto dust shalt thou return'.

Usage– Why keep running after money? After all, we will be *ashes to ashes and dust to dust.*

A shot in the arm

Encouragement; impetus.

Usage– The AIDS campaign got *a shot in the arm* when the big celebrities came forward to support it.

A sight for sore eyes

Something one is glad to see.

Usage– The lone restaurant on the deserted highway was *a sight for sore eyes.*

As yet
Up to this moment.

Usage– Shirin has not given any answer *as yet*.

At an arm's length
At a distance.

Usage– I try to keep my prying co worker *at an arm's length.*

At a Loss
To be unable to comprehend.

Usage– Father was *at a loss* to understand why Lokesh needed to steal money despite getting a good pocket allowance.

At a standstill
At a dead end; seeming to go nowhere.

Usage– The talks between the heads of the nation are again *at a standstill.*

At daggers drawn
Bitter enmity.

Usage– The rival tribes were *at daggers drawn*.

At fault
In the wrong.

Usage– Madhu was *at fault* in the entire episode.

A thing of beauty is a joy forever
A beautiful object pleases the viewer.

Usage– Ruma implored her father to buy her a red mustang, saying that *a thing of beauty is a joy forever*.

At a loss
Confused, puzzled.

Usage– The emotional farewell speech left Harish *at a loss for words*.

At a pinch

If necessary.

Usage– Shubhi doesn't like to do cooking, but she'll do it *at a pinch* if her husband asks her to cook something special for him.

At a stretch

Continuously.

Usage– Working on the computer *at a stretch* gave her a crick in the neck.

At cross pusposes

With contradictory effect.

Usage– I was regularly watering my empty flower bed which my gardener wanted to prepare for planting new saplings. We were working *at cross purposes*.

At death's door

On deathbed.

Usage– Chakri's grandmother realized that she was *at death's door* when she saw her face.

At every turn

All the time.

Usage– When Raghu joined medical college, he encountered problems *at every turn*.

At first glance

Just by looking.

Usage– I could make out *at first glance* that the young boy was interested in my sister.

At heart

Basic nature.

Usage– He looks tough, but he is very sensitive *at heart*.

At home in

Fully acquainted.

Usage– Aman feels *at home in* his sister's house.

At large

Free (usually for someone who should be captive).

Usage– The police announced a reward to catch the dreaded gangster who was *at large* after the robbery.

At liberty

Free to do anything.

Usage– The rich businessman's son is *at liberty* to pursue his hobbies.

At one fell swoop

Suddenly, in one action.

Usage– The eagle swept down and carried the little fish in her beak *at one fell swoop.*

At one's beck and call

To wait on someone.

Usage– Little Julie has an army of servants *at her beck and call.*

At the bottom of

At the core or source of.

Usage– Mark was *at the bottom of* the prank played on the Manager.

At the top of

With maximum force.

Usage– Shreyas screamed *at the top of* his voice.

Attend to

Pay attention to.

Usage– Father asked me to *attend to* my duties in a more responsible manner.

Attend on

To serve.

Usage– The King appointed an entourage of maidservants to *attend on* his favourite Queen.

Axe to grind

To serve a selfish purpose.

Usage– Stan presented the group project report as his individual effort; he always has his own *axe to grind*.

A to Z

Completely, thoroughly.

Usage– Sheila wanted to open a departmental store which would sell *A to Z* consumer goods.

•••

B

Babe in the woods

Naïve, innocent.

Usage– Chinni couldn't let her young teenage daughter go to the party unescorted because despite her airs she was just a little *babe in the woods.*

Backbite

Speak evil about someone in their absence.

Usage– My friend likes to *backbite* about the other students.

Backbone

Main support.

Usage– Ramesh is the *backbone* of his family.

Backward and forward

To and fro.

Usage– Fortune is never static; it keeps swinging *backward and forward.*

Back and forth

To and fro.

Usage– The new father was pacing *back and forth* in the corridor outside the operation theatre.

Back down

Change one's opinion or position.

Usage– The Shiv Sainiks had to *back down* in the face of immense public outrage.

Back handed

Indirect; implied.

Usage– My friend gave me a *back handed* compliment by calling me a spoilt brat.

Back to the drawing board

Make a new design or plan from scratch after the rejection of the first one.

Usage– It was *back to the drawing board* for the team when the management rejected their first draft of the plan.

Back off

Withdraw.

Usage– The attacker *backed off* when Dinesh pounced on him angrily.

Back out

To evade a commitment.

Usage– Himesh *backed out* of his business deal when the market went up.

Back waters

Remote, laidback area.

Usage– We planned a holiday in the tranquil *back waters* of Kerala.

Bad blood

Ill will; enmity.

Usage– There has been *bad blood* between the brothers after the father's death.

Bad books

In disgrace; out of favor.

Usage– Urvashi is in the *bad books* of her teachers because of her loose morals.

Bad debt

A debt which cannot be recovered.

Usage– I did not want to loan money to my sister, since I knew I would have to write it off as a *bad debt*.

Bad egg

Good for nothing; loser.

Usage– Dhruv is not really a *bad egg*, he's just gullible.

Bad mouth

To say nasty things about someone.

Usage– Zarina *bad mouths* just about any and everyone.

Bad patch

Difficult time.

Usage– Mallika's friends helped her through when her marriage hit a *bad patch*.

Bag and baggage

With all one's personal effects.

Usage– We left the country *bag and baggage* after the 1982 riots.

Bag of bones

An emaciated person or animal.

Usage– Cancer had reduced Asha to a *bag of bones*.

Baker's dozen

Thirteen in number.

Usage– "How many muffins, sir?" "Make it a *baker's dozen*, please."

Bald as a coot

Completely bald

Usage – Kirat's tutor is as *bald as a coot*.

Bandy words

To discuss; to exchange heated words.

Usage– Geet tried to *bandy words* with the lawyer in an effort to save the situation.

Bank upon

To rely on.

Usage– She *banks upon* her parents' advice.

Banner flying

Continue the work.

Usage– After Bhagat Singh's martyrdom, the other freedom fighters vowed to keep the *banner flying*.

Baptism by fire

A trying ordeal.

Usage– Joan of Arc's *baptism by fire* earned her sainthood.

Bark is worse then the bite

Someone whose angry words are worse than his actual deeds.

Usage– My supervisor's *bark is worse than his bite.*

Bark up the wrong tree

To follow the wrong scent.

Usage– The accused kept protesting the charges and told the investigating officer that he was *barking up the wrong tree.*

Basket case

An infirm or inefficient person or scheme.

Usage– Nipesh's brother is a *basket case,* and his company has finally fired him.

Basking in the glory of

Enjoying the credit for something.

Usage– The actor was *basking in the glory* of his highly successful father.

Bated breath

In anticipation.

Usage– I waited to hear my result with *bated breath.*

Batten down the hatches

Prepare for trouble

Usage – The poor monsoon did not augur well for the crop, and the farmer asked his farmhand to *batten down the hatches* and be prepared for the worst.

Be all and end all

The most crucial part, the final result.

Usage– My mother consoled me when I did not get through the IIM entrance exam saying that this exam was not the *be all and end all* of my career prospects.

Bear a hand

Give assistance.

Usage– I asked Kay to *bear me a hand* in lifting the heavy box.

Bear down on

Approach someone in a determined way.

Usage– The boys seemed to *bear down on* Rohan in an aggressive way.

Bear in mind

To remember, consider.

Usage– She wanted her son to *bear in mind* the repercussions of his actions.

Bear out

To corroborate; to confirm.

Usage– Jalil's cousin was not willing to *bear out* his false story.

Bear up

To keep up one's spirits, to endure.

Usage– You must *bear up* until the financial troubles are over.

Beard a lion in its den

To challenge a greater power on its own soil.

Usage– The British came for business to India and successfully *bearded the lion in its own den* by ruling her for about a century.

Beat about the bush

Approach a subject in an indirect manner; stray, digress.

Usage– My boss told me to get to the point since there was no use always *beating about the bush.*

Beat a retreat

To retreat.

Usage– When the goons advanced menacingly towards Harish, he thought it prudent to *beat a hasty retreat*.

Beat it

To withdraw or retreat.

Usage– Mother asked me to *beat it* when I started pestering her for another slice of the cake.

Beat the air

To fight a losing battle.

Usage– In fighting against poverty, our government seems to be *beating the air.*

Beat the living daylights out of someone

To beat or thrash someone.

Usage– The students *beat the living daylights out of* the eve teaser.

Bed of roses

An easy condition of comfort or luxury.

Usage– Father always said that life is not a *bed of roses.*

Bed fellows

A close friend.

Usage– Hunger and Honesty make unlikely *bed fellows.*

Been there done that

Experienced; seasoned.

Usage– All her horticulture advice fell flat when Komal realized that Shivani has *been there done that* all her life.

Behind one's back

During one's absence.

Usage– The staff signed a petition and sent it to the board *behind the back* of their ill tempered boss.

Before you could say Jack Robinson

Suddenly; in a very short time.

Usage – The wily politician changed his stance *before you could say Jack Robinson.*

Behind every great man there's a great woman

Literal.

Usage– Kasturba Gandhi's contribution to her husband's cause can never be trivialized; after all *behind every great man there's a great woman.*

Behind the scenes

In private.

Usage– The director invited guests on the sets of his new movie to get a feel of *behind the scenes* activity.

Bell the cat

Take the leading part in any dangerous job.

Usage– The Opposition wants to oust the President from power but nobody is ready to *bell the cat.*

Benefit of doubt

Favorable judgment when culpability is uncertain.

Usage– Shirish was set free because of the *benefit of doubt.*

Beside oneself

Having lost selfpossession.

Usage– When her child came back home safe, the mother was *beside herself* with joy.

Best of both the worlds

Enjoy the benefits of two situations.

Usage– The teacher advised Mark to pursue his passion in both soccer and music and enjoy the *best of both the worlds.*

Best foot forward

Impressive start, best beginning.

Usage– Zubin wanted to *put his best foot forward* when his inlaws called him over.

Best of my belief

To the best of my knowledge; so far as I know.

Usage– To the *best of my belief,* he is a reasonable man.

Better late than never

Literal.

Usage– Even if you start with your studies now it will be *better late than never.*

Better off

In superior circumstances.

Usage– People in the villages today are *better off* than urban dwellers when it comes to healthy living.

Between the devil and the deep blue sea

A difficult choice; in a desperate dilemma.

Usage– The girl's mother did not know whether to refuse or to allow her daughter to go unescorted to the party; she was caught *between the devil and deep sea.*

Between you and me

Secret.

Usage– *Between you and me,* I am leaving this job.

Bid goodbye

To take leave.

Usage– As soon as he heard his flight being announced, Lakshya *bade goodbye* to his friends.

Big apple

Nickname for New York, USA.

Usage– My trip to the *Big Apple* was a memorable one.

Big fish in a small pond

Important or influential in a limited circle.

Usage– The President of our Residents' Association commands respect because he is a *big fish in a small pond.*

Bill of fare

Menu card; list of dishes etc.

Usage– Titu asked the bearer to bring the *bill of fare* so he could order the meal.

Birds and bees

Facts about sex.

Usage– There is a right time to know about the *birds and bees,* and parents should make an effort to communicate openly with their children.

Bird's eye view

An overhead view.

Usage– We enjoyed the *bird's eyeview* of Delhi from the top of Qutab Minar.

Birds of a feather flock together

Like minded people tend to stick together.

Usage– There is no doubt why Komal and Shivani are friends; *birds of a feather flock together.*

Bite off more than one can chew

To take on more than one is capable of.

Usage– Naval tried to keep up with both MBA and CA, but soon he realized that he had *bitten off more than he can chew.*

Bite someone's head

Speak angrily.

Usage– Deepak was ready to *bite his son's head off* when he saw his new car's smashed fender.

Bite the bullet

Bear pain.

Usage– When Anita's only son moved out, she decided to *bite the bullet* graciously.

Bite the dust

Fall to the ground.

Usage– With the star's announcement of her engagement to a little known businessman, the story of her affair with her co star *bites the dust.*

Bite the hand feeds

Repay kindness with treachery.

Usage– The servant did not want to divulge information about his employer and *bite the hand that feeds him.*

Bitter end

To the last.

Usage– The brave soldiers fought to the *bitter end.*

Bitter sweet

Mixture of sweet and bitter.

Usage– Love is a *bitter sweet* experience.

Black and blue

Beaten severely.

Usage– The goons beat the young boy *black and blue.*

Black and white

In writing.

Usage– The management asked the union leader to submit their demands in *black and white.*

Black books

To incur someone's displeasure.

Usage– Sahil is in the *black books* of his teacher.

Black sheep

A worthless or disgraced member of the family

Usage – Sandeep was the *black sheep* of his family.

Blessing in disguise

A negative event with positive side effects.

Usage– Farid's termination from his job was a *blessing in disguise* because he soon started his own business.

Blood and iron

Relentless use of force.

Usage– Hitler ruled Germany through *blood and iron*.

Bloodhound

A detective.

Usage– Avinash is the *bloodhound* of the police force, and he loves his work.

Blood sucker

An extortionist.

Usage– The shopkeepers in my neighborhood are *blood suckers.*

Blow a fuse

Get angry.

Usage– The teacher *blew a fuse* when Niranjan refused to listen to him.

Blow hot and cold

To be indecisive, irresolute.

Usage– Focus and perseverance are important to achieve one's goals, one must not *blow hot and cold.*

Blow one's own trumpet

To praise oneself.

Usage– Ragini likes to *blow her own trumpet.*

Blow over

To pass away as a danger or scandal.

Usage– The star's publicity manager consoled him saying that the unpleasant scandal would *blow over* in the course of time.

Blow up

Explode.

Usage– The terrorists decided to *blow up* the factory.

Blunt the edge of

To weaken force.

Usage– Time has *blunted the edge* of Anoop's impatience and anger.

Body and soul

Wholly; completely.

Usage– Pablo Picasso was devoted to his art *body and soul.*

Body politic

Collective body of the people.

Usage– In a democracy, the leaders are guided by the *body politic.*

Boiling point

The point at which one becomes very angry.

Usage– David reached the *boiling point* when he saw the trainees sitting idle and chatting.

Bolt from the blue

Suddenly, out of nowhere.

Usage– The news of his girlfriend's unforeseen pregnancy came like a *bolt from the blue.*

Bone dry

Completely dry.

Usage– The clothes on the clothesline were *bone dry* by the evening.

Bone idle

Lazy, lethargic.

Usage– Vibhuti is *bone idle* and loves being a couch potato.

Bone of contention

Something that causes strife.

Usage– Money became the *bone of contention* in the businessman's family.

Bone to pick

A reason for conflict.

Usage– My hostile neighbor always has some or the other *bone to pick* with me.

Born with a silver spoon in one's mounth

Born rich.

Usage– Sunehri was *born with a silver spoon in her mouth* to the richest man in town.

Born under a lucky star

To be lucky.

Usage– John wins every racing bet; he is *born under a lucky star.*

Boot is on the other leg

The tables are turned.

Usage– Though the school bully had started the fight, he was beaten up by Raghav. He was not the only one facing punishment since *the boot was on the other leg* now.

Bosom pal

Best friend.

Usage– Sudha is my *bosom pal.*

Bread and butter

Earn a living.

Usage– Cars are Jimmy's passion as well as his *bread and butter.*

Break even

Equal profit and loss.

Usage– Manohar's business is barely managing to *break even.*

Break ground

Something new attempted for the first time.

Usage– The invention of the bulb *broke new ground.*

Break one's heart

Make sad.

Usage– His girlfriend's marriage with his friend *broke his heart.*

Break one's journey

Short stop en route a journey.

Usage– We decided to *break our journey* in Jaipur en route to Ajmer.

Break one's word

Break promise.

Usage– Mother was upset with Kavya for *breaking her word* and not returning home on time.

Break the ice

To get conversation going.

Usage– At the formal official party of her new office, Rita *broke the ice* by introducing herself to the other guests.

Breathe down one's neck

Watch every action closely.

Usage– In the small house, her sister in law was *breathing down her neck* the whole day.

Breathe one's last

On deathbed.

Usage– Deepika wanted to be there for her mother when she *breathed her last.*

Bring home the bacon

To earn one's living.

Usage– Kevin is the sole bread winner of his family, and he has to work hard to *bring home the bacon.*

Bring to book

Call to account.

Usage– All religious texts tell us that we will be *brought to book* for all our misdeeds.

Bring to light

Discover or expose.

Usage– The newscaster was awarded for *bringing the scam to light.*

Bring up

To raise a child; to speak up.

Usage– It is important to *bring up* children with love and respect.

Bring up the rear

To come last.

Usage– Our school's Red House *brings up the rear* in the school parade.

Bottle up

To enclose as in a bottle.

Usage– The counselor told the little boy that it was unhealthy to *bottle up* anger.

Bottomless pit
In hell.
Usage– Greed and avarice is a *bottomless pit.*

Bottom of one's heart
With heartfelt sincerity.
Usage– "We thank you from the *bottom of our heart* for what you have done for us," said the patient's family.

Brain wave
A sudden bright idea.
Usage– The committee had cornered Andrea when he had a *brain wave* which saw him through the emergency.

Bring about
Cause to happen.
Usage– Indira Gandhi *brought about* great changes in the country.

Bring down
To humble; to lower.
Usage– It is not nice to *bring down* your friends.

Brush away
To put aside.
Usage– He *brushed away* the rumors with a wave of his hand.

Brush up
Revive, freshen.
Usage– Please *brush up* your grammar before the entrance exam.

Buck up
Cheer up.
Usage– '*Buck up*! you are winning the race,' cheered the crowd.

Buckle down
Work seriously.
Usage– During exams Bhanu decided to *buckle down* and start studying seriously.

Build castles in the air
To plan impossible schemes.
Usage– Krish's father admonished him not to keep *building castles in the air* and take up a career seriously.

Bull in a china shop
Clumsy, awkward.
Usage– The villager was like the *bull in a China shop* in the elite gathering.

Burn a hole in one's pocket
Spend extravagantly.
Usage– The new cell phone has *burnt a hole in my pocket.*

Burn the candle at both ends
To waste quickly.
Usage– The boy *burnt the candle at both ends* by wasting money and gambling.

Burn the midnight oil
To work hard at studies.
Usage– Most students *burn the midnight oil* when the exams are round the corner.

Bury the hatchet
To make up, to give up enmity with someone.
Usage– It is high time Shakeel and Raza *bury the hatchet.*

Butt in
Interject, step in.
Usage– Father doesn't like it when he is speaking and I *butt in.*

Buy off

To bribe.

Usage– The prisoner *bought off* the jail superintendent.

By and by

Step by step; before long.

Usage– He will learn his duties *by and by*.

By and large

Generally speaking.

Usage– In the tribes the society is by and large matriarchal.

By leaps and bound

Rapidly.

Usage– The cancer had progressed *by leaps and bounds* in the last few months.

By hook or by crook

By fair or foul means.

Usage– Jerry wanted to get into college *by hook or by crook*.

By the dozen

Very many.

Usage– The hostess ordered muffins *by the dozen*.

By fits and starts

With many stops.

Usage– Charlie cannot be regular at the gym since he likes to exercise *by fits and starts*.

By the way

In passing.

Usage– *By the way*, what are you doing today evening?

•••

C

Cake and ale
All the good things of life.

Usage– Kanak has *cakes and ale* while her brother does not have even dry bread and water.

Call a halt
Order to stop.

Usage– The judge decided to *call a halt* to the proceedings.

Call a spade a spade
Speak plainly and bluntly.

Usage– Raja is quite blunt and is known for *calling a spade a spade.*

Call it a day
To quit working for the day.

Usage– When the bell sounded, Shraddha decided to *call it a day.*

Call attention to
Literal.

Usage– Let me *call attention to* your project which was submitted quite late.

Call of the wild

Appeal of nature.

Usage– Aamir wanted to respond to the *call of the wild* by going to the sanctuary.

Call someone's bluff

To ask someone to prove.

Usage– Watan *called his friend's bluff* by telling him to eat hundred muffins as he had boasted.

Capital sentence

Death as punishment.

Usage– The court awarded a *capital sentence* to Prateik for the murder.

Carbon footprint

The amount of carbon dioxide emitted; contribution towards global warming.

Usage– My school project deals with the importance of reducing our *carbon footprint* in an effort to trim down the environmental hazards.

Cards on the table

One's moves to be fully transparent.

Usage– Ambuja put all his *cards on the table* before signing the business deal.

Carrot and stick

Reward and punishment.

Usage– The project teacher used the *carrot and stick* approach to get the students to take more interest in their projects.

Carry away

Emotional, deprive of self-control.

Usage– Julia got *carried away* by her husband's emotional speech and admitted to her affair.

Carry coal to new castle
Take a thing where it is in abundance.
Usage– Importing Yoga from the West is like *carrying coal to Newcastle.*

Carry on
Manage to continue.
Usage– His son will *carry on* the business after his death.

Carry one's cross
To live with pain or trouble.
Usage– Kind words from family and friends make it easier for us to *carry our cross.*

Carry out
Accomplish.
Usage– The thief *carried out* the theft as per the plan made by his associate.

Carry the day
To be successful.
Usage– Nitin's bright ideas *carried the day* in the annual general meeting.

Carry too far
To continue beyond reasonable limits.
Usage– It is sensible not to *carry quarrels too far*.

Carry through
To support through difficulties.
Usage– Faith *carries you through* all obstacles.

Carry weight
To have influence or authority.
Usage– My advice *carries no weight* with my mother in law.

Cart before the horse

To reverse the natural order of things.

Usage– Don't plan your accessories before deciding your dress; it is like putting the *cart before the horse.*

Carve out

To gain by one's exertions.

Usage– You must *carve out* a career for yourself.

Cast a horoscope

To make an astrological calculation.

Usage– The pundits *cast my horoscope* for matrimonial purposes.

Cast anchor

To anchor a ship.

Usage– The naval ship *cast anchor* in Mumbai.

Cast a spell on

To enchant.

Usage– The speaker *cast a spell on* the listeners.

Cast a vote

Record one's vote.

Usage– To whom are you *casting your vote*?

Cast off

Wearing handed down clothes.

Usage– Dinesh is wearing his son's *cast offs.*

Cast the first stone

To be the first to blame someone.

Usage– Tahir should have looked at his own past before trying to *cast the first stone* on Shaadab's character.

Cat and dog's life
Full of quarrels.

Usage– Gina's married life has been more of a *cat and dog's life* than a bed of roses.

Catch as catch can
Using any means.

Usage– Haneef's *catch as catch can* approach to his professional life has landed him in trouble.

Catch hold of
To catch, seize.

Usage– The police *caught hold of* the treasure hidden by the wily thief.

Catch someone red handed
Catch someone in the act of doing wrong.

Usage– The accountant *caught the manger red handed* taking the bribe from the client.

Catch sight of
See.

Usage– Imam could not *catch sight of* his friend in the crowd.

Catch up
To overtake; to be on par with.

Usage– The neighbors found it difficult to *catch up with* the fashionable Rahejas.

Cat's paw
Tool of another person.

Usage– Riteish has been his father's *cat's paw* in the business.

Cave in
To slip.

Usage– The news showed laborers trapped inside the mine which had *caved in* due to heavy rains.

Chalk and cheese

Dissimilar.

Usage– The twins are as different as *chalk and cheese.*

Chalk out

To formulate.

Usage– My secretary will *chalk out* my schedule for the day.

Chance upon

Find out by chance.

Usage– He *chanced upon* his friend's address in the old school book.

Change one's tune

To change one's thinking or words.

Usage– After suffering losses in the share market, Yogesh *changed his tune* about the necessity of investing in shares.

Chapter and verse

Complete information.

Usage– The manager knew the details of the entire episode, *chapter and verse.*

Charity begins at home

Literal.

Usage– Anahita likes to feed poor people regularly rather than going to fancy NGO events because she believes that *charity begins at home.*

Cheek by jowl

Side by side.

Usage– The sisters had lived *cheek by jowl* all their lives.

Chew the cud/fat

To chat in a friendly way.

Usage– My friend and I can *chew the cud* for hours.

Chicken hearted

A coward.

Usage– Tinu is a *chicken hearted* fellow.

Chicken and egg

Used for a situation where one doesn't know which came first.

Usage– When the two children fought, I did not know how the fight had begun; it was a *chicken and egg* situation.

Chickens come home to roost

Bad deeds or words return to haunt

Usage – When Dhritrashtra saw how adamant Duryodhana was to wage war on his cousins, he knew that *chickens had come home to roost.*

Child's play

Easy.

Usage– Manu needs to take studies seriously; after all IAS exams are not a *child's play.*

Chip off the old block

Quite like the father.

Usage– The ace golfer's son is a *chip off the old block.*

Choke up

Fill completely.

Usage– Her heart was *choked up* with emotion.

Chuck it

Stop; give up.

Usage– You have been wasting time sitting idle; just *chuck it* and do something worthwhile.

Chuck up

To give in; to leave.

Usage– After the scam he decided to *chuck up* his job and go to the US.

Clear off

To go away.

Usage– The guard shouted, "*Clear off* from here. This is private property and you are trespassing!"

Clear out

To get rid of; to empty.

Usage– Amod was single handedly responsible for *clearing out* the inefficient officers from the police force.

Clear the air

Ease up the situation and relieve tension.

Usage– The minister must *clear the air* about his involvement in the incident.

Clear the way

Make the way open.

Usage– His brother's marriage *cleared the way* for his own.

Clear up

To make or become clear.

Usage– The police wanted to *clear up* the mystery of the journalist's murder as soon as possible.

Clip the wings

Restrain ambition, bring under control.

Usage– Sonia's mother in law knows how to *clip the wings* of her career ambitions.

Cloak and dagger

Furtive and secretive.

Usage– I hate all this *cloak and dagger* stuff about meeting my boyfriend secretly.

Close in upon

Surround and draw in.

Usage– The policemen *closed in upon* the gang of bandits.

Close quarters

In close contact with.

Usage– The manager hated the star because he had seen her at *close quarters* and knew what a shrew she was.

Cloud nine

Blissful; happy

Usage– Belinda was on *cloud nine* when the date of her wedding was fixed.

Coast is clear

There is no obstacle or danger in the way.

Usage– The army was ordered to proceed as the *coast was clear*.

Cock and bull story

An unbelievable story.

Usage– The child tried to get out of the situation by spinning an improbable *cock and bull* story.

Cold blooded

Without feeling.

Usage– He was sentenced for the *coldblooded* murder of the young girl.

Cold Comfort

Less consolation, aid or comfort than one needs.

Usage– Her distant behavior was *cold comfort* for my frazzled nerves.

Cold Feet

Loss of nerve or confidence.

Usage– The band's leader got *cold feet* just before the big stage performance.

Cold shoulder

Aloof or distant.

Usage– Veena was hurt when her friend gave her the *cold shoulder* at the party.

Cold war

Silent war; war without words.

Usage– The *cold war* between the two friends had gone on for a long time.

Come clean

To confess; to divulge everything.

Usage– Kanav *came clean* in the court and was acquitted.

Come about

Happen.

Usage– Nothing great ever *comes about* without great effort.

Come across

Meet.

Usage– Ila *came across* an old friend in the market

Come back to earth

To get real; to stop imagining.

Usage– Our teacher asked Samuel to stop dreaming and *come back to earth.*

Come full circle

To come back to the starting point.

Usage– Our cultural values and thinking have *come back full circle* after decades of Western influence.

Come hell or high water

Whatever may come; regardless of obstacles.

Usage– Tina has decided that, *come hell or high water,* she will try hard and be selected in the school team.

Come into

To fall heir to.

Usage– He *came into* a large estate.

Come round

To change one's opinion.

Usage– The young girl *came round* when the boy pleaded and entreated her again and again.

Come of age

Reach legal age.

Usage– Ritu exclaimed that she has *come of age* and could come from the party any time she wanted to.

Come to grief

Face trouble or disappointment.

Usage– Too much pride *comes to grief* sooner or later.

Come to one's senses

Act sensibly.

Usage– Arushi has finally *come to her senses* after being under Dharam's spell for a long time.

Come to the point

Not digress.

Usage– The director asked the project manager to stop wasting time and *come to the point.*

Come to a standstill

To come to a stop.

Usage– The train *came to a standstill* much before the station.

Come to blows

To fight.

Usage– After the heated discussion, the two young men *came to blows.*

Come to light

To reveal.

Usage– With the reporter's efforts many little known facts have *come to light* now.

Compare notes

Exchange experiences and impressions.

Usage– After our holiday in the US, my friend and I enjoyed *comparing notes.*

Cook one's goose

Finish off; kill; to ruin.

Usage– The testimony of the witness against the accused was enough to *cook his goose.*

Cook the books

Distort accounts.

Usage– Sahid was questioned by the auditors regarding the *cooking of their books.*

Contempt of court

Interference with the administration of justice.

Usage– The judge found Tony guilty of the *contempt of court.*

Cool one's heels

To be kept waiting.

Usage– He was made to *cool his heels* in the minister's office.

Count one's chicken before they're hatched

Count profit before earning it.

Usage– The author was dreaming of the Booker Prize even before his novel was published; he was clearly *counting his chicken before they were hatched.*

Counting sheep

Distracting oneself to sleep by counting imaginary sheep.

Usage– Vivek is a chronic insomniac and even *counting sheep* does not help any more.

Count upon

To depend.

Usage– One can always *count upon* one's parents.

Cover one's tracks

Not to leave any traces.

Usage– Though the thief had *covered his tracks* well, the police found him in no time at all.

Cream of the society

The richest people in town.

Usage– The *cream of the society* was present at the high society wedding.

Creature comforts

Material luxuries.

Usage– Today the attainment of *creature comforts* has become more important than spiritual evolvement.

Crop up

Happen unexpectedly.

Usage– Since he refused to change his working pattern, the problem of finding a job *cropped up* now.

Cross one's fingers

As a sign of good luck.

Usage– Mini *crossed her fingers* before entering the room for her interview.

Cross one's mind

Occur.

Usage– It did *cross my mind* that Hussain may not want to see me.

Cry over split milk

Bemoaning what cannot be undone.

Usage– When Utkarsha cried on seeing her result, her mother told her that there was no use *crying over split milk.*

Cut above

Something distinctly better.

Usage– Milka Singh, also known as 'The Flying Sikh', was a *cut above* the other athletes.

Cut and dried

Readymade; clear cut.

Usage– She offered a *cut and dried* strategy to handle the issue of plummeting sales.

Cut and run

To be off quickly.

Usage– Pooja decided to *cut and run* when she saw the principal coming from the other side.

Cut corners

To take a short cut.

Usage– The teacher instructed us to do our project sincerely without trying to *cut corners.*

Cut down to size

To prove that someone is not as good as he thinks.

Usage– When the leader kept boasting about his achievements, the news reporter *cut him down to size* by pointing out the riots which had taken place in his tenure.

Cut in

To force one's way in.

Usage– The uncouth boy *cut in* ahead of the other car to take the last parking slot available.

Cut off without a shilling

To bequeath nothing.

Usage– Romesh's father *cut him off without a shilling.*

Cut one's coat according to one's cloth

To adapt oneself to one's financial circumstances.

Usage- She asked her friend to curb her expenses and *cut her coat according to her cloth.*

Cut one's losses

To reduce losses.

Usage– The good trader needed to work out a strategy to *cut his losses.*

Cut out for it

Fit or apt for.

Usage– Harjeet is *cut out for* a soldier's life.

Cut short

Abridge, reduce.

Usage– Arti had to *cut short* her holiday.

Cut both ways

To be equally applicable for and against.

Usage– His arguments *cut both ways.*

•••

D

Damp squib
Disappointing

Usage– The old students' meet turned out to be a *damp squib*.

Dance attendance on
To wait on someone.

Usage– The people around the minister were happy to *dance attendance* on him.

Danger line
The border line between danger and safety.

Usage– Ankur is so foolhardy that at times he does not even realize that he has reached the *danger line*.

Dark continent
Africa.

Usage– My trip to the *Dark Continent* was full of fun and adventure.

Dark horse
An unexpected or surprise winner.

Usage– The young candidate turned out to be a *dark horse* when he won the elections.

Dark ages

The earlier period of history; the Stone Age.

Usage– During the *dark ages,* survival was the biggest challenge that man faced.

Dash off

Produce hastily.

Usage– He *dashed off* a letter to the director.

Dash out

Rush out.

Usage– She *dashed out* as soon as her work was done.

Day in and day out

For a long time.

Usage– I see him working in the garden *day in and day out.*

Dead as a dodo

Completely dead.

Usage– There was no mistake about it, the dog was *dead as a dodo.*

Dead as a doornail

Unusable, lifeless.

Usage– The mouse was *dead as a doornail.*

Dead of night

In the middle of the night.

Usage– The thieves broke into the house in the *dead of the night* and stole the whole cash.

Dead loss

A complete loss.

Usage– The books drenched in the rain were a *dead loss* to the shopkeeper.

Debt of honor

Debt not recognized by law but by one's word.

Usage– Every *debt of honor* must be paid.

Deliver the goods

To carry out what is required or promised.

Usage– Though the promos of the movie were quite good it failed to *deliver the goods* at the box office.

Deny oneself

To refuse to allow oneself gratification; to exercise selfdenial.

Usage– The great ascetic *denied himself* comforts and luxuries to set a right example before the masses.

Devil of a mess

Very bad mess.

Usage– The world economy today is in a *devil of a mess*.

Devil's advocate

One who pleads the wrong cause.

Usage– The lawyer who defended the dreaded terrorist was no less than the *devil's advocate.*

Devil to pay

Serious trouble ahead.

Usage– The principal warned Harshita that if she did not mend her ways she'd have the *devil to pay* later in life.

Die away

To disappear by degrees; become gradually inaudible.

Usage– The noise of the firecrackers *died away* in the distance.

Die down

To subside.

Usage– All false rumours *die down* in the course of time.

Die hard

To die with great struggle.

Usage– Old habits *die hard*.

Die is cast

An irrevocable step has been taken; there is no turning back now.

Usage– Once the results are put up on the notice board, the *die is cast*.

Die out

To become extinct; to disappear.

Usage– With largescale construction going on everywhere, the green belt is slowly *dying out*.

Different kettle of fish

A different thing altogether

Usage – Manan had hosted parties for his friends in college days, but he knew that organizing an official party was a *different kettle of fish*.

Dilly dally

Be indecisive; to procrastinate.

Usage–He kept trying to *dillydally* even when he knew that a quick decision was unavoidable.

Dime a dozen

Easily available and therefore of little value.

Usage– Tortoise shell artifacts are available a *dime a dozen* at the seafront curio shop.

Disappear into thin air

Vanish.

Usage– The first information report from the police file had *disappeared into thin air*.

Discretion is the better part of valour

It is better to be cautious than to be foolishly brave.

Usage– It was a tough decision for Ankur to back off from the goons, but after all, discretion *is the better part of valour.*

Dispense with

Terminate; give.

Usage– The chemist *dispensed with* the medicines.

Dissolved in tears

Weeping copiously.

Usage– When his brother snatched his ice cream, little Chang *dissolved in tears.*

Divine right of the Kings

Right to rule as they like.

Usage– The Egyptian Pharaohs enjoyed the *divine right of Kings* and complete and unquestioned obedience from the subjects.

Do away with

Abolish; kill.

Usage– It is high time our government decides to *do away with* the archaic British laws.

Do a double take

Look again in awe and wonder.

Usage– When I saw the urchin wearing a new coat, I *did a double take.*

Do up

Make tidy; decorate.

Usage– Daya wanted to *do up* the guest room well in time for his guests.

Do well

To prosper.

Usage– Many villagers leave their homes and come to cities, but only some of them *do well* here.

Dog in the manger

Mean, spiteful.

Usage– Anand's old man is a *dog in the manger.*

Dog's chance

Little chance.

Usage– We don't have a *dog's chance* to win this match.

Dog's life

To lead a wretched or miserable life.

Usage– The slaves in the Middle Ages led a *dog's life.*

Donkey's years

A long time.

Usage– Harsh and Bunty have been friends for *donkey's years.*

Don't change horses in midstream

Do not abandon a project mid way.

Usage– Mother insisted on continuing with the same tutor, convinced that one should *not change horses in midstream.*

Don't have a clue

To have no idea.

Usage– "Do you know why Vikrant has left his job?" "I *don't have a clue.*"

Don't keep a dog and bark yourself

Literal.

Usage– Shaan's mother does all the housework herself despite having servants; wasn't it rather like *keeping a dog and barking yourself.*

Don't look a gift horse in the mouth

Don't undervalue a gift.

Usage– Rudaali likes to know the worth of the gifts she gets. Apparently, no one has ever told her that one should *not look a gift horse in the mouth.*

Double dealer

Deceitful person.

Usage– The minister's aide turned out to be a *double dealer* as he was accepting bribes from the opposition leader.

Double edged

Striking both ways.

Usage– Raja's argument was *doubleedged,* and managed to satisfy both the parties.

Double minded

Undecided.

Usage– You should not be *doubleminded* about your career.

Double up

To bend over with laughter.

Usage– When Pankaj cracked a joke, everybody *doubled up.*

Double whammy

A double blow or setback

Usage – It was a *double whammy* for Shweta when her new servant broke his hand after her old and trusted servant left.

Down and out

At the end of one's resources.

Usage– Clare's family was *down and out* and he could not afford to lose his job.

Down on one's luck

Illluck.

Usage– Bhavna was keen to help her cousin when he was *down on his luck.*

Drag on

To go on as such.

Usage– The lawyer advised Sheila to settle the case out of court rather let it *drag on* for years.

Draw a blank

Get no results.

Usage– The research did not throw any light on the subject, and the team had to report that they had *drawn a blank.*

Draw near

Approach.

Usage– Myra's birthday is *drawing near.*

Draw the line

Define a limit.

Usage– Madhur allows his son to take a drink with him, but *draws the line* soon thereafter.

Dress down

To scold; to wear casual or informal clothes.

Usage– The principal called the pranksters and gave them a *dressing down.*

Dress up

To dress elaborately.

Usage– The bridegroom was *dressed up* for the occasion.

Drink in

To absorb.

Usage– Sandy *drank in* the whole scene at the pub before reaching for a drink.

Drop dead gorgeous

Very beautiful.

Usage– The new model looks *drop dead gorgeous* in the advertisement.

Drop in the bucket/ocean

A very small quantity.

Usage– The big businessman's donation helped the NGO, but it was only a *drop in the bucket.*

Drop a curtsy

To curtsy.

Usage– The young girl *dropped a curtsy* when the Queen arrived.

Drop in

To come casually.

Usage– I asked Manoj to *drop in* whenever he was in the town.

Drop off

Fall asleep.

Usage– Most of our classmates *dropped off* in the bus on the way to Nainital.

Drop out

To disappear from one's place; give up.

Usage– Many students who do not do well in studies *drop out* before finishing graduation.

Drop a hint

To give an indication.

Usage– The teacher *dropped a hint* about the carnival dates.

Drop on one's knees

Humble oneself.

Usage– The beggar *dropped on his knees* before the woman who gave him food.

•••

E

Eagle eyed

Keen sighted.

Usage– The *eagle-eyed* policeman caught the thief trying to escape.

Ear to the ground

To be well informed; to know how things are.

Usage– The manager has an *ear to the ground* and knows exactly what is going on.

Early bird catches the worm

One who starts early is more successful.

Usage– Vishaka wanted to fill the form of the entrance exam as soon as the date was announced, since she firmly believed that an *early bird catches the worm.*

Easy circumstances

Affluence.

Usage– Yogesh is lucky to be a man of *easy circumstances.*

Easy come easy go

Money acquired without effort and spent thoughtlessly.

Usage– Sachin does not value his ancestral property, for him it is *easy come easy go.*

Easy going

Relaxed; comfortable life.

Usage– Thanks to her rich father, Nisha had always had an *easygoing* life.

Easy money

Money made without much labour.

Usage– The young nowadays do not want to toil hard, they just want to make *easy money.*

Ease off

Slacken gradually.

Usage– Her knee pain *eased off* after taking the pain killer.

Easy virtue

Loose character.

Usage– The girl in question is of *easy virtue.*

Eat away

Gnaw gradually; destroy.

Usage– Grief *eats away* the stoutest of hearts.

Eat humle pie

Admit an error or mistake.

Usage– Shruti had to *eat humble pie* when despite her mother's warnings she drove the car and crashed straight into the side wall.

Eat like a horse

To eat hungrily.

Usage– The young boy *ate like a horse* after the cricket match.

Eat one's cake and have it too

To use and still have something.

Usage– By working from home, the young mother felt she could *eat her cake and have it too.*

Eat one's hat

An undertaking promised on conditions which one thinks very improbable.

Usage– If despite his casual approach Umesh manages to score well in exams, I will *eat my hat.*

Eat one's heart out

To pine away.

Usage– It was there for all to see that the grief stricken young widow *ate her heart out.*

Eat one's words

To retract; recant.

Usage– When Tanisha performed well in all the entrance exams, her tutor had to *eat his words.*

Eat up

Devour completely; consume; absorb.

Usage– The youngsters *ate up* the entire bowl of pudding.

Edge in a word

To get a word in with difficulty.

Usage– When the discussion about the policy was underway, the soft spoken Abhay tried in vain to *edge in a word.*

Egg on

To encourage, urge or induce.

Usage– He *egged me on* to answer back and insult our teacher.

Eleventh hour

In the nick of time; at the very last moment.

Usage– The police served a subpoena on the main witness at the *eleventh hour*.

Empty handed

Bringing no gift.

Usage– He came to his friend's house *emptyhanded*.

Englishman's home is his castle

A man's home is his refuge

Usage – The poorest man feels safe and secure in his humble abode; after all, an *Englishman's home is his castle.*

Enough and to spare

In sufficient quantity.

Usage– The rich industrialist can give charity since he has money *enough and to spare*.

Enter into

To become a party to.

Usage– Elesh refused to *enter into* any agreement without consulting his lawyer.

Escape one's notice

To overlook.

Usage– The accountant admitted that the computing error had *escaped his notice*.

Evening of life

Old age.

Usage– My parents are now enjoying the *evening of life.*

Ever and anon

From time to time.

Usage– Farida comes to my house *ever and anon.*

Evergreen

Always fresh.

Usage– The beauty and charm of traditional South Indian saris is *evergreen.*

Every dog has his day

Everyone gets a chance.

Usage– Raseel is very popular with the nouveau riche nowadays, well, I guess, *every dog has his day*

Every now and again

Now and then.

Usage– In the initial years the friends' new business faced troubles *every now and again.*

Every now and then

At intervals.

Usage– My friends and I like to meet over a cup of coffee *every now and then.*

Every other

Every second or alternate.

Usage– I go to my friend's house *every other* day.

Every which way

Every way.

Usage– He tried *every which way* to woo the girl of his dreams.

Exception that proves the rule

Literal.

Usage – If God made a rule that all birds must fly, then He also made flightless birds like ostrich as an *exception that proves the rule.*

Eye for an eye

Complete revenge.

Usage– Gandhiji said that an *eye for an eye* will make the whole world blind.

Eye in the back of one's head

Ability to know what is happening behind one's back.

Usage– My warden has *eyes in the back of her head* for nothing we do ever escapes her notice.

Eyes pop out

Shocked, surprised.

Usage– Sundari's *eyes popped out* when she saw her daughter in the movie hall during school hours.

•••

F

Face like thunder

Annoyed; angry.

Usage– Jay's *face looked like thunder* when his boss pointed out his past misdemeanors.

Face off

Either an actual or figurative confrontation.

Usage– The *face off* between the two players resulted in one being eliminated.

Face that launched a thousand ships

Beautiful woman; coined for Helen of Troy.

Usage– Cleopatra was legendary for having a *face that launched a thousand ships*.

Face the music

To accept unpleasant consequences at their worst.

Usage– The boys who had bunked classes had to *face the music* when they were caught.

Face to face

In actual presence.

Usage– The two warring gangsters met *face to face* in the court.

Fact of the matter

The plain truth.

Usage– The *fact of the matter* is that children are the worst victims of divorce.

Fade away

To disappear gradually.

Usage– Vibha hoped her scars would *fade away* with time.

Fair and square

Honest.

Usage– Zahir is very *fair and square* in all his business dealings.

Fair means

Honestly.

Usage– We won the game by *fair means*.

Fair play

No cheating.

Usage– Mother encouraged us to adopt *fair play* in everything we did.

Fair weather friends

Selfish friends, only for the good times.

Usage– One should keep away from *fairweather friends*.

Fair sex

Female sex; women.

Usage– Our boss declared that the *fair sex* would not be given any special treatment by the management.

Fairy godmother

Someone who gets you out of trouble.

Usage– I am sick of playing my erring friend's *fairy godmother* all the time.

Faith will move mountains

Literal.

Usage– When little Zoya got the baby sister she had been praying for, her mother was not one bit surprised; after all, *faith will move mountains*.

Fall back

To retreat; to go for help.

Usage– Retired folk have to *fall back* on their reserves.

Fall flat

To fail.

Usage– All his efforts to pacify the two parties *fell flat*.

Fall for

To be enamored of; to be taken in by.

Usage– Romeo *fell for* Juliet as soon as he set eyes on her.

Fall foul

To come in conflict.

Usage– The boy *fell foul* of his friends.

Fall from grace

To fall from a high position.

Usage– The minister's *fall from grace* was followed by his unceremonious exit.

Fall guy

Scapegoat.

Usage– Poor Somesh always ends up becoming the *fall guy* and taking the blame for his brother's pranks.

Fall head over heels

Fall in love.

Usage– Neelam has *fallen head over heels* in love with her fiancé.

Fall short

In short supply; not up to the required or expected mark.

Usage– Sugandha's academic performance *fell short* of the teacher's expectations.

Fall over backwards

Try hard to please someone.

Usage– The new daughter in law *fell over backwards* trying to please her new family.

Fall a prey

To become a victim.

Usage– The little boy *fell prey* to the pedophile's vile intentions.

Fall out

To have differences; quarrel.

Usage– The two brothers *fell out* after their father's death.

Fancy free

Without ties or commitments.

Usage– Ramanna has no intentions of getting married; he is happy to be *fancy free* and foot loose.

Far fetched

Having distant meaning.

Usage– His reason seemed too *far-feched* to be true.

Far sighted

Capable of seeing to a great distance.

Usage– My father's sound investments prove that he is a *far sighted* man.

Fat is in the fire

A critical act which precipitates trouble.

Usage– Now that one of the boys has confessed to the crime, *the fat is in the fire.*

Father of the Nation

Mahatma Gandhi.

Usage– Gandhiji, the *Father of the Nation,* gave his life and blood to our country.

Feather in one's cap

A striking distinction.

Usage– Winning the academy award was yet another *feather in the director's cap.*

Feather one's nest

To accumulate wealth for oneself while serving others in a position of trust.

Usage– The government officer has *feathered his nest* comfortably in his tenure.

Feel at home

To feel at ease or comfortable.

Usage– Alvira tried to make us *feel at home* when we went to visit her.

Feel the pinch

Suffer shortage.

Usage– With rising inflation, the middle class *feels the pinch.*

Feel the pulse

To find out the trend of one's thought.

Usage– Before taking any decision the government wanted to *feel the pulse* of the masses.

Female of the species is more deadly than the male

Literal.

Usage– My father warned me to be careful of my female boss, adding that the *female of a species is more deadly than the male.*

Field day

A day of excitement.

Usage– The children had a *field day* at the carnival.

Fifteen minutes of fame

Short spell of recognition

Usage – The struggling actress agreed to appear in a no holds barred reality show to enjoy her *fifteen minutes of fame.*

Fifty fifty

Equally.

Usage– We have a *fifty fifty* chance of winning the match.

Fight it out

Struggle on until the end.

Usage– Mother wanted Norma to *fight it out* with her friends rather than come home and complain.

Fight shy of

To avoid.

Usage– He *fights shy of* controversies and conflicts.

Fight someone tooth and nail

Fight with all one's might.

Usage– The Pandavas *fought their cousins tooth and nail* in the war.

Fill in

To occupy especially time; to add what is necessary to complete.

Usage– My brother *filled me in* on all that I had missed when I was away.

Find one's feet

To be able to provide for oneself.

Usage– Anupama realized that she could *find her feet* only after finishing her studies.

Find out

Discover; detect.

Usage– She *found out* about her husband's affair from the newspaper.

Fine arts

Arts like painting, sculpture and music.

Usage– Dwija wanted to pursue *fine arts* as a career option.

Fine feathers do not make fine birds

Literal.

Usage– Vandana may dress well but that does not make her a good friend; *fine feathers do not make fine birds.*

Finger in the pie
A share in the doing of anything.
Usage– He is such a meddlesome character that he wants a *finger in every pie.*

Fingers and thumbs
Awkward, clumsy.
Usage– The old woman is all *fingers and thumbs.*

Finger licking delicious
Delicious food.
Usage– Harjinder's mother makes *finger licking delicious* biryani.

Fire and brimstone
Wrath; extreme irritation.
Usage– He was full of *fire and brimstone* with his inept brother in law.

Fire and sword
Devastation.
Usage– Freedom was achieved under *fire and sword.*

Fire away
Begin.
Usage– My boss asked me to *fire away* when I got my research report.

First and foremost
The most important.
Usage– The *first and the foremost* thing for anyone seeking employment is to learn computers.

First come, first serve
To be obliged on one's turn.
Usage– The doctor's secretary told the patient that the doctor saw patients on *first come, first serve* basis.

First hand information

Information got through one's own self.

Usage– The news reporter relies only on *first-hand information* for his reports.

Fish out of water

A person who feels uncomfortable in his surroundings.

Usage– While traveling abroad, I felt like a *fish out of water.*

Fit and starts

Irregularly.

Usage– My car sputtered up in *fits and starts.*

Fit out

Equip.

Usage– The bus operator instructed the showroom to *fit out* the bus for the tour.

Fit as fiddle

In the best condition.

Usage– The doctor pronounced the young man to be as *fit as a fiddle.*

Flash in the pan

A one time achievement.

Usage– The athlete wanted to win every race and prove that his medal was not just a *flash in the pan.*

Flat rate

A fixed uniform rate.

Usage– According to the Indian government's order sugar is sold at a *flat rate* in the country.

Flee for one's life

To run away and save one's life.

Usage– During the riots many people had to *flee for their lives* and relocate.

Flesh and blood

In person; relatives.

Usage– Uma was happy to see her cricket idol in *flesh and blood.*

Flow with milk and honey

Prosperous.

Usage– In ancient times, India was referred to as 'The Golden Sparrow' and it was known as the land which *flowed with milk and honey*

Fly in the ointment

Some slight flaw which corrupts a thing of value.

Usage– Nisha's mother was a *fly in the ointment* in the whole program.

Fly off the handle

Become angry.

Usage– My next door neighbor tends to *fly off the handle* whenever we pluck flowers from his garden.

Fly the coop

Run away, escape.

Usage– The young prisoner *flew the coop* by giving bribe to the police officers.

Foam at the mouth

Become angry.

Usage– The mention of her exhusband's name still makes Diksha *foam at the mouth.*

Follow in the footsteps

To follow the example of.

Usage– Rajvir Singh wants to *follow in the footsteps* of his father and become a politician.

Follow suit

To do what another has done.

Usage– When Myra went to Europe for a holiday, her brother decided to *follow suit.*

Food for thought

Something which forces one to think.

Usage– His articles always provide *food for thought.*

Fool and his money are soon parted

Literal

Usage– When Amber invested all his savings in stocks and shares, his brother thought, "Oh well! A *fool and his money are soon parted."*

Fool around

Playing or handling carelessly.

Usage– Mother asked me not to *fool around* with the knife lest I cut my finger.

Fool's paradise

A state of false expectation.

Usage– If Sara thinks that she can win the tennis match without adequate practice, she is living in *fool's paradise.*

Foot in the grave

To be on the point of death.

Usage– My grandmother has one *foot in the grave,* yet she is quite cheerful.

Foot the bill

Pay the expense.

Usage– Ambika's brother agreed to *foot the bill* of her medical expenses.

Forbid the banns

Make formal objection to a marriage.

Usage– When Jenny announced her marriage to Rick, she did not anticipate that her ex boyfriend would *forbid the banns*.

Forbidden fruit

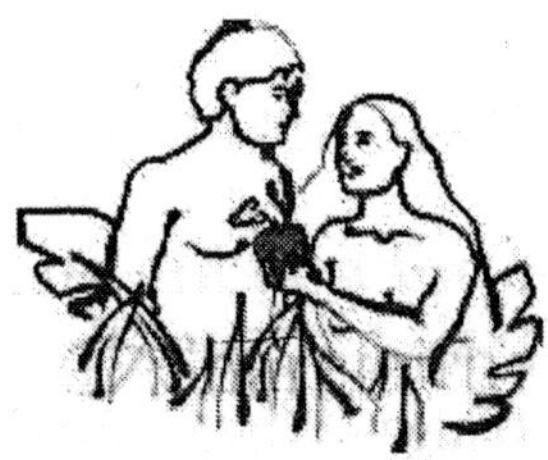

Anything tempting but prohibited.

Usage– Even though Jacob knew that Sarita was a married woman, he could not resist her; *forbidden fruit* surely is the sweetest.

Force one's hand

To make one do something earlier than planned.

Usage– Vanita did not want to take up a job, but dire financial need *forced her hand.*

For ever and a day

Forever; always.

Usage– Jim and Jenny had known each other *for ever and a day*.

Foregone conclusion

An inevitable conclusion.

Usage– When Sachin Tendulkar played in full form and hit one six after another, the result of the match soon became a *foregone conclusion*.

Foul play
Dishonest dealing.

Usage– Though the student's death looked like suicide, the police did not rule out *foul play.*

Four corners of the earth
Anywhere; everywhere.

Usage– Buddha wanted the message of peace to prevail in the *four corners of the earth.*

Frame of mind
Mindset; mood.

Usage– I did not go for my career counseling session today since I am not in the proper *frame of mind.*

Free hand
Complete freedom of action.

Usage– With my mother in law away, I am enjoying a *free hand* in the kitchen.

French leave
To proceed on leave without permission.

Usage– The government officers in my colony are fond of availing *French leave.*

Fresh lease of life
New scope for living.

Usage– We got a *fresh lease of life* when we migrated to Australia.

Fret and fume
To be angry with; to be cross.

Usage– There is no use *fretting and fuming* about something as common-place as a traffic jam.

From door to door

From house to house.

Usage– The salesman makes his living selling wares *from door to door*.

From hand to mouth

To live within a little income.

Usage– The middle class in India today are living *from hand to mouth*.

From pillar to post

From one place to the other.

Usage– Digvijay ran from *pillar to post* trying to get a job.

Fuddy duddy

Stuffy or old fashioned.

Usage– My uncle is a dear old *fuddy duddy*.

•••

G

Gain ground
To make progress, move ahead.
Usage– Peace and disarmament is *gaining ground* in world politics.

Gain on or upon

To overtake by degrees.
Usage– The athlete gradually *gained upon* his closest contender in the last lap of the marathon.

Gain time
To get time on some pretext.
Usage– The minister issued an ambiguous statement for the general public in order to *gain time.*

Gall and wormwood
Anything extremely disagreeable.
Usage– I found the women's gossip all *gall and wormwood*.

Gallop through
To make quick progress.
Usage– Neeraj *galloped through* the hierarchy to reach the top position of his company.

Game is afoot

A game is in progress.

Usage– Ranbir could not leave the stadium while the *game was afoot.*

Game is not worth the candle

The benefits are not worth the labor and expense.

Usage– Misogynists believe that marriage is a *game not worth the candle.*

Game is up

The scheme has failed; to be found out.

Usage– When the police reached the spot, the thief realized that the *game was up.*

Game that two can play

Literal.

Usage– When Pinto pushed his junior's plan as his own, he forgot that this is a *game that two can play.*

Gang up on

To join together; act as a group.

Usage– The children *ganged up* against the bully who had threatened their friend.

Generation gap

Literal.

Usage– The differing viewpoints of a father and son can be ascribed to the *generation gap* between the two.

Gate crasher

Uninvited intruder at a party.

Usage– The *gate crashers* at Obama's party are all set to appear in a television show.

Gather ground

Make progress; find a foothold.

Usage– By and by he has *gathered ground* in the new office.

Gather oneself together

To compose oneself.

Usage– The new intern tried to *gather herself together* before the board meeting.

Gear up

To increase the pace; make the speed higher.

Usage– The director urged the students to *gear up* for the examination.

Gentleman's agreement

An agreement resting on honor and not any formal contract.

Usage– Aarav honored the contract with Timmy even though it was only a *gentleman's agreement* and there was nothing on paper.

Gentleman's gentleman

Valet.

Usage– Joseph has been a *gentleman's gentleman* for the last two decades.

Get ahead

Make progress.

Usage– Shirish wants to *get ahead* in his career on his own steam.

Get around

Move about.

Usage– Word tends to *get around* pretty fast in a small town.

Get away with murder

Not be punished.

Usage– Raghav is so charming and persuasive that he can *get away with murder.*

Get a word in edgewise

To find a chance to say.

Usage– The soft spoken girl tried to *get a word in edgewise* in the noisy discussion.

Get by

To be able to go past.

Usage– The old widow manages to *get by* on her meager pension.

Get even

To owe nothing; to seek revenge.

Usage– Naushad wants to *get even* with Roshan for stealing his notebook.

Get going

To begin or move.

Usage– Mother asked Anushka to leave the television couch and *get going.*

Get in someone's hair

Annoy someone.

Usage– Donna loses her cool when her mother nags her and *gets into her hair.*

Get in someone's act

Make oneself a part of an ongoing act.

Usage– My manager was not interested in our research, but during the presentation *he got in on our act* to take all the credit.

Get into shape

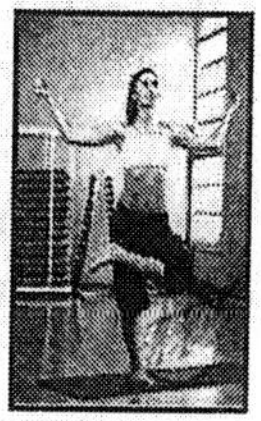

To get fit.

Usage– The new mother decide to join a gym to *get into shape.*

Get off the ground

Get a good start.

Usage– Asin had toiled hard to *get the project off the ground.*

Get one's own back

Have one's revenge.

Usage– Yasmin is always criticizing my dress sense, but I *got my own back* when she was pulled up by our teacher for dressing inappropriately.

Get on one's nerves

Irritate or annoy.

Usage– The grating sound of the glass cutter *got on my nerves.*

Get out

To free oneself.

Usage Pinki tried everything to *get out* of the sticky situation.

Get over

To surmount; to recover from.

Usage– Prahlad could never *get over* the financial losses he had incurred.

Get over with

Finish.

Usage– Shreyas cannot wait to *get over with* his exams.

Get the sack

Fired from job.

Usage– Our deputy manager *got the sack* when the company head decided to lay off surplus staff.

Get thee behind me Satan

Jesus' reply to Devil, someone who is trying to tempt.

Usage– Guddi saw the packet of chips on her table, and murmured to herself, '*Get thee behind me Satan.*'

Get the feel of

To get used to.

Usage– There were no classes on the first day of college so the students could *get the feel of* the campus.

Get the show on the road

To start a program.

Usage– The director approved of our project and urged us to *get the show on the road.*

Get the worst of

To be defeated, to lose.

Usage– Rani Laxmibai was prepared to *get the worst of* British warfare tactics, and geared herself for a grueling battle.

Get through

To pass through.

Usage– My spirituality helps me to *get through* troubled times.

Get through to

To be able to understand.

Usage– The interpreter tried her best to *get through to* the Korean ambassador.

Get to first base

To make a good start.

Usage– The girls took Arvind's phone number and were glad to *get to first base.*

Get to the bottom of

To find out the truth.

Usage– The police were keen to *get to the bottom of* the scam as soon as possible.

Get to the point

Come to the important part.

Usage– The manager was impatient for the trainee to *get to the point.*

Get under one's skin

Bother, upset.

Usage– My niece shrieked and protested when I took her to the doctor's and *got under my skin.*

Get up on the wrong side of the bed

To wake up in a bad temper.

Usage– My coach must have *got up on the wrong side of the bed* today since he just kept shouting at us right through the match.

Get used to it

Accept a particular fact.

Usage– Anjali is trying to *get used to* the idea of settling in the US.

Get your dander up

Become annoyed.

Usage– When my younger brother threw a tantrum, mother asked me to be patient and not *get my dander up*

Get your goat

Irritate or annoy.

Usage– It really *gets my goat* to see people misbehaving with beggars.

Giddy goat
Behave foolishly
Usage – Herman's aunt acted quite the *giddy goat* when she met his fiancée for the first time.

Gift of the gab
Ability to talk well.
Usage– The salesman who sold me two suitcases really had the *gift of the gab.*

Gilt edged securities
Those stocks whose interest is considered perfectly safe.
Usage– My father believes in investing only in *gilt edged securities.*

Gird up one's loins
To prepare for action.
Usage– Just before the battle, the General asked his battalion to *gird up their loins* and be prepared for the worst.

Give a hard time
To give trouble.
Usage– The new baby was *giving Ragini a hard time.*

Give and take
Reciprocity, fair exchange.
Usage– All friendships are based on equal *give and take.*

Give away
To give for nothing; to donate.
Usage– He *gave away* his house to the NGO to be made into a shelter for the poor.

Give as good as someone get

Defend oneself, to pay back in equal measure.

***Usage*–** Though Deepu is youngest of the siblings, he still *gives as good as he gets.*

Give chase

Pursue.

***Usage*–** The police *gave chase* to the robber.

Give ear

Listen.

***Usage*–** The teacher asked the students to *give ear* to the whole story.

Give free rein to

Give freedom to do as one wishes.

***Usage*–** Madhu decided to *give free rein to* her daughter in law to run the house.

Give in to

Yield.

***Usage*–** The management *gave in to* the demands of the employees' union.

Give one's right arm

To give something extremely valuable in return for something.

***Usage*–** Any struggling artist would *give their right arm* for a break like this.

Give one's word

Promise.

***Usage*–** She *gave her word* that she would not divulge my secret to anyone.

Give someone enough rope and he will hang himself

Literal.

Usage– The police detective let the accused talk without interrupting him. Experience had taught him that if you *give a criminal enough rope he will hang himself.*

Give someone the benefit of doubt

Literal.

Usage– The lawyer requested the judge to *give his client the benefit of doubt* in the absence of tangible proof.

Give the devil his due

To be fair to someone one doesn't like.

Usage– Ritika is lazy, but to *give the devil his due,* she does manage to submit all her projects on time.

Give the game away

Reveal the truth.

Usage– Though Suresh kept denying his affair, his little black diary *gave the game away.*

Give the glad eye

Welcoming look; appraising glance.

Usage– Damini's brother in law always *gives her the glad eye* when she walks into the room.

Give the slip

Escape.

Usage– The boy's warden was taking them to the headmaster's office but they *gave him the slip.*

Give up

Abandon.

Usage–They *gave up* the whole enterprise after it failed for the second time.

Give way

To make room.

Usage– The soldiers *gave way* to the ladies in the ballroom.

Go about one's business

To attend to one's affairs.

Usage– She saw her old neighbor *go about his business* regularly and diligently.

Go berserk

Behave frenzied or violent.

Usage– The old woman *went berserk* and started hitting out at the people standing around her.

Go getter

Active and ambitious person.

Usage– Ritwik has been a *go getter* and is now running a successful business.

Go haywire

Become deranged.

Usage– She saw her mother *go haywire* after her father's untimely demise.

Go the whole hog

Go to the full extent.

Usage– Political leaders *go the whole hog* to win elections.

Go through

To perform; read.

Usage– The teacher asked her students to *go through* the book.

Going to hell in a hand basket

On a course towards disaster.

Usage–Arshad's obsession with his friend's wife is ruining his married life; he is *going to hell in a hand basket.*

Gone with the wind

Gone forever.

Usage– The days of the humble typewriter have *gone with the wind.*

Go one's own way

Do what one wants to do.

Usage– When the couple realized that they could not live together any more, they decided to *go their own way.*

Go out of one's ways

To make an extra effort.

Usage– Jennifer *goes out of her way* to help her friends.

Go out on a limb

Put oneself in an isolated or disadvantaged position to support someone or something

Usage– The politician's supporters decided to *go out on a limb* and support his protest march.

Go overboard

Be fond or overenthusiastic.

Usage– Sangeeta *went overboard* with the arrangements for her daughter's marriage.

Go round in circles

Keep attempting to do something without reaching the finish point.

Usage– The mathematical problem was so complex that Eddie kept *going round in circles.*

Go through the motion

Pretend to be doing something.

Usage– I saw Vaishali *going through the motions* of doing the housework, but her mind was clearly somewhere else.

Go to pieces

Break up entirely.

Usage– Sulabha feared that her daughter would *go to pieces* if her husband died.

Go without saying

To be plainly selfevident.

Usage– It *goes without saying* that good academic scores will ensure admission in the best of colleges.

Gold digger

One who is bent upon making money through all means.

Usage– Koel is a *gold digger.*

Good for nothing

Useless; worthless.

Usage– Salim is *good for nothing.*

Grease one's palm

Bribe.

Usage– The government officers are infamous for doing their work only if you *grease their palm.*

Grind one's own axe

To serve one's self-interest.

Usage– I thought that Kusum was interested in social service, but all this while she was just trying to *grind her own axe.*

Grow on

To gain a greater hold on.

Usage– The taste of exotic cheese *grows on* you gradually.

Guardian angle

Literal.

Usage– Vaibhavi's *guardian angel* must have been by her side the day she survived the terrible car crash.

Guinea pig

A subject of an experiment.

Usage– Patients are quite often used as *guinea pigs* in hospitals to try new drugs and medicines.

•••

H

Hairy at the heel
Dangerous and untrustworthy.

Usage– Jayesh is *hairy at the heel* and none of his friends trust him.

Half and half
A mixture of two equal things.

Usage– This cocktail is beer and brandy *half and half.*

Half baked
Inexperienced, an unplanned idea.

Usage– The girl's idea was so *half baked* that her teacher dismissed it without even considering it.

Half hearted
Lacking courage.

Usage– She made a *half hearted* effort to resolve the conflict.

Hand in glove
Extremely close.

Usage– The juvenile delinquent worked *hand in glove* with the local policeman.

Hand in hand

Working together closely.

Usage– The Marketing and Finance team worked *hand in hand* on the new project.

Hand to mouth

Poverty.

Usage– The thief confessed that he had taken to crime because he was sick of his *hand to mouth* existence.

Hand and foot

To attend to someone.

Usage– The servant waited on his old master *hand and foot.*

Hands down

With utter ease.

Usage– The Indian hockey team won the match *hands down.*

Handwriting on the wall

A foreshadow of disaster.

Usage– The pre election opinion polls made the ruling party see the *handwriting on the wall.*

Hang by a thread

A small chance.

Usage– His selection in the school team *hangs by a thread* on the whims of the coach.

Hanged for a sheep as for a lamb

Literal.

Usage– The little girl took the candy along with all the cookies in the jar, thinking that she might as well be *hanged for a sheep as for a lamb.*

Hang in the balance

To be in doubt or suspense.

Usage– The promotion of the senior staff *hangs in the balance* till the new CEO takes charge.

Hang one's head

To feel ashamed.

Usage– The little boy *hung his head* when his mother scolded him.

Hang out to dry

To abandon or not support.

Usage– If Swaroop doesn't become serious soon, his team manager is going to *hang him out to dry*.

Hang over one's head

To be in danger.

Usage– The death threat *hanging over the cricketer's head* made it imperative to have adequate security around him.

Hang heavy

Become burdensome.

Usage– After his retirement, he found time *hanging heavy* on his hands.

Hanky panky

Jugglery; underhand trickery.

Usage– Sarita rebuked Om and told him not to try any *hanky-panky* with her.

Happy-go-lucky

Easy going.

Usage– Skand is a *happy-go-lucky* fellow.

Hard and fast

Strict.

Usage– There is no *hard and fast* rule in becoming a member of the City Library.

Hard facts

Undeniable facts.

Usage– Poverty and unemployment are two very *hard facts* about India and they cannot be ignored.

Hard hearted

Cruel.

Usage– My sister is quite *hard-hearted.*

Hard nut to crack

Difficult problem to solve.

Usage– The scientist realized that the problem of increasing the agricultural output was a *hard nut to crack.*

Hard of hearing

Deaf.

Usage– The old couple was *hard of hearing.*

Hard up

In want of money.

Usage– Illis is *hard up* ever since he lost his job.

Hat trick

Three successes in a row.

Usage– Titu scored a *hat trick* in the cricket match.

Have a ball

To have a great time.

Usage– We *had a ball* at the New Year's bash.

Have a bone to pick

Have a reason to quarrel.

Usage– Kamini *has a bone to pick* with everyone around her.

Have a heart

To be kind and sympathetic.

Usage– I asked Kiran to *have a heart* when she slapped her little girl for some small mistake.

Have the best of both the worlds

Literal.

Usage– Students working part time can *have the best of both the worlds.*

Have the last laugh

To make someone look foolish.

Usage– Sudhir *had the last laugh* when despite a low academic score he got a seat in the college of his choice.

Have your heart in your mouth

Feel fear or terror.

Usage– The young mother's *heart was in her mouth* when she saw her little girl trying to climb out of the cradle.

Hawk eyed

Keen-sighted.

Usage– Very little misses the *hawk eyed* old security man of my building.

Head is in the clouds

Unrealistic or impractical.

Usage– Shloka's *head is in the clouds* and he never has a realistic plan for the future.

Head on the block

To be held responsible if something goes wrong.

Usage– It will be Sunidhi's *head on the block* if anything goes wrong with this project.

Head to foot

All over the body.

Usage– In the Middle East, Muslim women have to stay covered from *head to foot*.

Head or tails

Guesswork.

Usage– The group of friends decided to do *head or tails* when they couldn't decide between a movie and picnic.

Hear, hear

An exclamation of approval from the listeners of a speech.

Usage– 'Hear, hear,' murmured the audience when the leader announced his plans to stabilize the economy in the coming year.

Heart and soul

With great devotion.

Usage– He served his master *heart and soul*.

Heart misses a beat

Suddenly shocked or surprised.

Usage– Suparna's *heart missed a beat* when she saw her ex boyfriend at the party.

Heart of hearts

Deep within one's heart.

Usage– Nicole may say that she hates her husband, but in her *heart of hearts* she still wants to reconcile with him.

Heart to heart

Frank and open conversation.

Usage– I enjoyed the *heart to heart* chat with my friend.

Heavy handed

Use force or authority.

Usage– The policeman was *heavy handed* with the thief.

Hell to pay

Unpleasant consequences.

Usage– Anuradha knew that she would have *hell to pay* if her mother found out about her boyfriend.

Hell has no fury like a woman scorned

Literal

Usage – Draupadi incited the Pandavas to fight against the Kauravas; after all, *hell has no fury like a woman scorned.*

Helter skelter

In a confused hurry; tumultuously.

Usage– The army ran *helter-skelter* when the enemy dropped a bomb on them.

Here and there

Aimlessly.

Usage– "Why are you wandering *here and there*?" asked my teacher.

Higgledy piggledy

Haphazard; in confusion.

Usage– The cows are running *higgledy-piggledy* on the farm.

High and dry

Stranded without help.

Usage– The employees were left *high and dry* when the CEO sold the company.

High and low

Everywhere.

Usage– He searched *high and low* for the right actress for his movie.

High and mighty

Exalted; arrogant.

Usage– Mary behaved *high and mighty* with the new girl in the class.

High on the hog

Affluent and luxurious.

Usage– The lord of the manor was *high on the hog*.

High spot

An outstanding feature.

Usage– The beautiful sunset was the *high spot* of our trip to the beautiful hill station.

High tea

Lavish and formal tea with snacks etc.

Usage– I was invited for *high tea* at the American embassy.

High time

Quite time when something was done.

Usage– It is *high time* you got married.

Hit below the belt

Unfair and mean attack.

Usage– It is unmanly to *hit below the belt*.

Hit rough weather

Difficulties.

Usage– The new project *hit rough weather* as soon as it was launched.

Hit the bull's eye

To be exactly right.

Usage– Sara *hit the bull's eye* when she said that her maid was looking like a pregnant woman.

Hit the roof

To lose temper.

Usage– Father *hit the roof* when my brother told him that he had decided to move to the US.

Hit the jackpot

To be lucky or successful.

Usage– The young entrepreneur has *hit the jackpot* with his innovative business idea.

Hit the nail on the head

To be right.

Usage– Mohan *hit the nail on the head* when he said that the core of all business problems was employee dissatisfaction.

Hit the sack

Go to bed.

Usage– Harmeet wanted to *hit the sack* the minute he reached home.

Hit upon

To come up; discover; devise.

Usage– Sir Isaac Newton *hit upon* his Theory of Gravity while idling in the apple orchard.

Hither and thither

Here and there.

Usage– When I reached home I found all that my sister had scattered all my clothes *hither and thither*.

Hobson's choice

No real choice at all

Usage – The defendant knew he was being offered the *Hobson's choice* of turning state witness or going to jail.

Hocus pocus

Jugglery; deception.

Usage– Aseem did not want to be involved in any *hocus pocus* that was going on in his office.

Hold forth

To put forward; to show; to speak in public.

Usage– Few orators can *hold forth* as well as Hitler could.

Hold the baby

To be left in the lurch with a responsibility.

Usage– When Prime Minister Jawaharlal Nehru died, Shri Lal Bahadur Shastri was left *holding the baby*.

Hold the torch

To have an unspoken or unrequited love for someone.

Usage– My brother still *holds the torch* for his Economics teacher.

Hold your own

Maintain one's position.

Usage– Vineet can *hold his own* in any discussion regarding his company.

Hold your tongue

To keep silence.

Usage– It is important to know when to speak and when to *hold your tongue.*

Hold together

Remain united.

Usage– Suman tried to *hold her family together* after her mother died.

Hold up

To bring to standstill; to stop and rob.

Usage– He is *holding up* the entire traffic on this road.

Hold up one's head

To face the world with self respect.

Usage– The old man had invested in a pension plan so that he could *hold up his head* and not be dependent on any one.

Home and hearth

Literal.

Usage– The memory of his *home and hearth* kept him toiling hard in the foreign land.

Honesty is the best policy

Literal

Usage – There is truth in the old adage that *honesty is the best policy.*

Honours are even

A match which ends in a draw.

Usage– The match was quite interesting even though by the end the *honors were even.*

Hook, line and sinker

To accept a story completely.

Usage– People fell for his story *hook, line and sinker.*

Hop, skip and jump

Only a short distance away.

Usage– My college is *hop, skip and jump* away from my house.

Hope against hope

To continue to hope even when all ground is gone.

Usage– We are *hoping against hope* that once the recession is over, the prices of essential commodities will go down.

Horns of dilemma

In a difficult situation.

Usage– I was on the *horns of dilemma* whether to tell the truth or to make a story.

Horses of a different color

A different matter.

Usage– Caste bias and reservation for the underprivileged are *horses of a different color.*

Hot air

Empty talk.

Usage– The leaders' plans of socialism are all *hot air.*

Hot and bothered

Anxious and worried.

Usage– Liam looked all *hot and bothered* when his mother asked him where he had been all day.

Hot under the collar

To be angry or bothered.

Usage– The policeman's rude handling made him *hot under the collar.*

Hot water

A state of trouble.

Usage– He spends more than he earns, and so finds himself in *hot water* ever so often.

Hour of need

Literal.

Usage– My parents have been always been by my side in my *hour of need.*

House of ill fame

Brothel.

Usage– You should stay away from *house of ill fame.*

House of cards

Ill planned; not strong.

Usage– Kunta's business turned out to be a mismanaged *house of cards* and Rakesh left it just as soon as he could.

Hue and cry

Great clamor; great noise.

Usage– There is a great *hue and cry* about celebrity paychecks nowadays.

Hunky dory

Satisfactory; fine

Usage – The tabloids reported that things are now *hunky dory* between the star couple.

•••

I

Icing on the cake

Literal.

Usage– Shrujan was so happy with his board exam's result, and the gift from his father was like *icing on the cake.*

Idle mind is a devil's workshop

Literal.

Usage– Balbir needs to be doing something now that he is retired; an *idle mind is a devil's workshop.*

If at first you don't succeed try, try again

Literal.

Usage– Mother asked me not to give up trying when I failed the driving test, saying that, *'If at first you don't succeed try, try again.'*

If it ain't broke, don't fix it

If something is working sufficiently well, leave it alone

Usage – When Hari saw his gardener trying to repair the old, but functional, lawn mower, he told him, *"If it ain't broke, don't fix it."*

If Mohammed won't come to the mountain, the mountain must come to the Mohammed

Literal.

Usage– If the tutor is not coming to Aryaman's house, then he'll have to go to the tutor's house for tuitions. After all, *if Mohammed won't come to the mountain, the mountain must come to the Mohammed.*

If wishes were horses beggars would ride

Wishing is not the same as getting something.

Usage– Prateik would love to ride a Harley Davidson, but of course, *if wishes were horses beggars would ride.*

If worst comes to worst

In the worst case scenario.

Usage– *If worst comes to worst*, Kajal will have to start working to fund her own education.

If you can't stand the heat, get out of the kitchen

Remove yourself from the situation you cannot handle.

Usage– Madan found it stressful to be a construction foreman. His wife told him, *'If you can't stand the heat, get out of the kitchen.'*

If you fly with the crows, you get shot with the crows

One's association with anything involves both its rewards and disadva-ntages.

Usage– Chadha's high profile friends got him into trouble with the police for drug dealing; *if you fly with the* crows, *you get shot with the crows*

I'll cross the road/bridge when I come to it

Literal.

Usage– If I don't clear my entrance exam I'll have to think of an alternate career choice. But *I'll cross the road when I come to it*.

I'll eat my hat

To be absolutely sure that one is right.

Usage– If Aftab gets that job, *I'll eat my hat.*

Ill at ease

To be uneasy.

Usage– Kanav was *ill at ease* in the company of the theatre artists.

Ill gotten gains

Illegal or unfair profit.

Usage– Darla has made a huge mansion with her *ill gotten gains*.

In a fix

In trouble.

Usage– Afzal was *in a fix* when he had to decide whether to tell his teacher the truth or be loyal to his friend.

In a jam/pickle

In trouble.

Usage– Salim was *in a jam* when the thief confessed that he had given him bribe.

In a jiffy

Something which happens quickly.

Usage– When asked about which dress she wanted, Anupama made up her mind *in a jiffy.*

In a nutshell

In brief.

Usage– Yousuf narrated the incident *in a nutshell.*

In another's shoes

Literal.

Usage– Niku did not want comment on her friend's choices for she had not walked *in her shoes* to know what had prompted her to make them.

In broad daylight

Openly; during the day.

Usage– The robbers had made a daring attempt *in broad daylight.*

In cahoots

Conspiring together.

Usage– The salesman and the accountant were *in cahoots.*

In donkey's years

For a very long time.

Usage– I haven't worn a mini skirt *in donkey's years* now.

In for a penny, in for a pound

Go the whole way and take all the risks.

Usage– Though Anil did not have any knowledge of stocks, he decided to follow his consultant's advice and go *in for a penny, in for a pound.*

In high spirits

In good mood.

Usage– The group of youngsters was *in high spirits* in the pub.

In one ear and out the other

To ignore.

Usage– Whatever mother says goes *in my sister's one ear and out the other.*

In so many words

Exactly as stated.

Usage– Nakul told Paru that he did not want to marry her, though not *in so many words.*

In stitches

Laughing uncontrollably.

Usage– The movie had us *in stitches.*

In the bag

Secured or as good as secured.

Usage– Manisha has the contract with the music company *in the bag.*

In the clear

No longer suspected of wrongdoing or crime.

Usage– Emon is *in the clear* now that the real thief has been caught.

In the dock

On trial.

Usage– Shivam was *in the dock* for killing his wife.

In the driver's seat

In charge or in control of a situation.

Usage– Abhijeet likes to be *in the driver's seat* in his relationships.

In the flesh

To actually meet someone.

Usage– Mahesh was ecstatic to meet his idol *in the flesh.*

In the long run

Over a long period of time.

Usage– Sudesh knows that only hard work pays *in the long run.*

In the offing

Very likely to happen.

Usage– Reports confirmed that the marriage of the two stars was *in the offing.*

In the pink

In good health.

Usage– George is *in the pink* of health.

In the pipeline

Something whose arrival is expected.

Usage– Our director told us about the other project which was *in the pipeline.*

In the red

An overdrawn bank account.

Usage– Tia's business has been *in the red* for the last one year now.

In the same boat

In the same situation.

Usage – All the traders were *in the same boat* after the government increased the excise duty.

In the swing

Good progress.

Usage – The preparations for Mansi's wedding were *in the swing* when her brother reached home.

In the zone

To be focused.

Usage – The young girl was *in the zone* about her future as a doctor.

In two minds

Undecided.

Usage – Scott was *in two minds* about going for a holiday at this time of the year.

In your element

To be one's best.

Usage – The comedian was *in his element* at the show.

Inside out

Literal.

Usage – The police officer had studied criminal psychology *inside out*.

Into each life some rain must fall

Bad or unfortunate things happen to everyone.

Usage – The priest consoled the orphan, saying that *into each life some rain must fall* before he can reach the rainbow.

Into thin air

To disappear.

Usage– The thief disappeared *into thin air.*

Iron in the fire

To have a number of things working at the same time.

Usage– Bhushan has many *irons in the fire* now that he is a partner in the firm.

It never rains but it pours

Literal.

Usage– Raashi lost her pen after spoiling her exam; *it never rains but it pours.*

It takes a village to raise a child

Literal.

Usage– The young singer was the pride of his small town; after all, *it takes a village to raise a child.*

It's not the size of the dog in the fight, it's the size of fight in the dog

Literal.

Usage– Aditi looks petite but she is an ace karate champion; *it's not the size of the dog in the fight, it's the size of the fight in the dog* which matters.

Itching palm

Greed for money.

Usage– The government officer's *itching palm* would have to be scratched before he would do the work.

Ivory tower

A place of retreat from the world; detached from the harsh realities of life.

Usage– A philosopher lives in an *ivory tower*.

•••

J

Jack of all trades

One who can turn his hand to any job.

Usage– Arvind is a *Jack of all trades* can always manage to earn his own living.

Jar upon

To irritate.

Usage– The noise of the blaring music *jarred upon* my nerves.

Jay walker

One who walks on road without paying any heed to traffic rules.

Usage– *Jay walking* on the road leads straight to hospital.

Jazz up

Brighten up.

Usage– Gunjan *jazzed up* her simple dress with bright accessories.

Jekyll and Hyde

Dual personality.

Usage– Hamza has a *Dr. Jekyll and Mr. Hyde* nature in that he can get really unpleasant when he is angry.

Jitterbug

One addicted to dancing.

Usage– My children have been bitten by the *jitterbug*.

Job's comforter

One who aggravates the distress of the unfortunate man he has come to comfort.

Usage– Swarna is my *Job's comforter,* but I still think only of her whenever I am distressed.

Jog trot

A slow but regular walk.

Usage– He enjoys his *jog trot* every morning.

Jog my memory

Usage– I *jogged my memory* to remember his name.

Johnny on the spot

A person who is ready and available to do something.

Usage– Ritesh started his career as a *Johnny on the spot* for the big production house.

Johnny come lately

A recent recruit.

Usage– Adam showed his sales graph to the *Johnny come lately* in a bid to inspire him.

Joined at the hip

Very closely connected.

Usage– The two friends are *joined at the hip.*

Jolly good fellow

A very social and popular fellow.

Usage– Krishna is a *jolly good fellow,* and has many friends at the club.

Jolly roger

The pirates' black flag with a skull and cross bones.

Usage– The ship came flying a *Jolly Roger.*

Judas kiss

False love.

Usage– He knew his wife's love was nothing more than a *Judas kiss.*

Jump at

To accept with eagerness.

Usage– The boys *jumped at* the opportunity to make easy money.

Jump down one's throat

To attack, to criticize.

Usage– Shram *jumped down my throat* when I told the teacher about him.

Jump on the bandwagon

Join.

Usage– Nitya decided to *jump on the bandwagon* and join the dance class with the rest of her friends.

Jump one's bail

To abscond, forfeiting one's bail.

Usage– Salman *jumped his bail* not realizing the consequences of his action.

Jump the gun

Start doing something before the appropriate time.

Usage– The manager asked the new intern not to *jump the gun* and wait his turn.

Jump through hoops

To make a great effort.

Usage– The maid was ready to *jump through hoops* to get the job.

Jump to conclusion

Form judgment quickly.

Usage– The detective asked the police officer not to *jump to conclusions* before the investigation was complete.

Jury's out

No general agreement or consensus .

Usage– The *jury's out* on whether the world will come to an end in 2012 or not.

Just desserts

To get the punishment one deserves.

Usage– The minister got his *just desserts* when he was voted out of office.

Just for the heck of it

Literal.

Usage– Sienna was not serious about sports; she played badminton *just for the heck of it*.

•••

K

Kangaroo court

A self appointed group who takes the law into their own hands and form courts that are not legal.

Usage– The mob held a *kangaroo court* and decided to kill the traitor.

Keen as mustard

Very enthusiastic.

Usage– The boys were as *keen as mustard* to be successful in life.

Keep an eye on

Watch.

Usage– Payal asked me to *keep an eye on* the child.

Keep body and soul together

To earn a living.

Usage– It is not easy to *keep body and soul together* on my meager salary.

Keep company

To be a companion.

Usage– He *keeps company* with the top politicians of our country.

Keep distance/at an arm's length

Stay away from.

Usage– She wanted to *keep distance* from the gossiping women.

He likes to *keep* her *at an arm's length.*

Keep it under your hat

Keep it secret

Usage – Arnika told her friend about her engagement, but asked her to *keep it under her hat.*

Keep mum

Keep quiet.

Usage– Akbar decided that he would not *keep mum* about his friend's involvement.

Keep tabs on

To keep a check on; to keep account of.

Usage– The concerned father wanted to keep tabs on the activities of his young son.

Keep up appearances

To keep up a superficial outward show.

Usage– Everybody around us is trying to *keep up appearances* these days.

Keep up with the Joneses

To try to be better than the neighbors.

Usage– It is futile to try and *keep up with the Joneses.*

Keep your ear to the ground

Try to stay informed.

Usage– It is the manager's business to *keep an ear to the ground.*

Keep your head above water

Managing to just about survive financially.

Usage– The car mechanic can barely manage to *keep his head above water* on his salary.

Keep your nose to the grindstone
To work hard and seriously.
Usage– Amarjit *keeps his nose to the grindstone* to earn enough to provide good education to his children.

Keep your shirt on
To tell someone to calm down.
Usage– The salesman told the young man who was arguing with him to *keep his shirt on* and not lose his cool.

Keyed up
Raised pitch or standard; stimulated.
Usage– Bhushan *keyed up* the party with his lively jokes.

Kick the bucket
To die.
Usage– The children of the rich man waited for him to *kick the bucket.*

Kick up dust
To create trouble.
Usage– The little boy's confession *kicked up dust* for everyone else involved.

Kill the goose that lays the golden egg

Literal.
Usage– When Roop fought with his boss he *killed the goose that was laying golden eggs.*

Kill two birds with one stone
To do two things with the means needed for one.
Usage– Manohar *killed two birds with one stone* when he took his family for the business trip.

Kill time
To waste time.
Usage– He went to the mall just to *kill time.*

Kith and kin

Near and dear ones.

Usage– I am quite fond of my *kith and kin.*

King of beasts

The lion.

Usage– The *king of beasts* looks majestic.

King of metals

Gold.

Usage– The *king of metals* has become so expensive that it is going to be seen only on kings now.

Knee jerk reaction

An instant reaction.

Usage– Jerry's denial was more of a *knee jerk reaction* than a statement.

Knight in shining armor

Someone who saves someone in danger.

Usage– Naushad was my *knight in shining armor* and he had swept me completely off my feet.

Knock out

Dislodge by a blow.

Usage– Though Lakshya is physically weak, he *knocked out* Sudipto's tooth with a blow.

Knock the bottom out of

To make ineffectual; to bring to a naught.

Usage– Repeated failure has *knocked the bottom out of* his ambition.

Knock your socks off
To be amazed or surprised.

Usage– It *knocked my socks off* to see my little girl performing so well on stage.

Know the ropes
Understand the details of procedure.

Usage– The junior clerk in the builder's office *knows the ropes* and has agreed to help me.

Know which side one's bread is buttered
To know where one's interest lies.

Usage– Taylor doesn't want to annoy his dean; he *knows which side his bread is buttered.*

Know your onions
To be experienced or knowledgeable about

Usage– Raghu has been a photographer for 20 years now and *knows his onions.*

Know which way the wind blows
To understand changing circumstances and to be able to anticipate the future accordingly.

Usage– My father encouraged me to make my own decisions, and said, "You don't need to be a weatherman to *know which way the wind blows.*"

Knuckle down
Get down to work and apply oneself earnestly and vigorously to it.

Usage– After the holidays, Arshad decided to *knuckle down* and begin work in all earnest.

Knuckle under
Give way; give in; submit

Usage– Vidya *knuckled under* the pressure of her parents and opted for MBBS.

•••

L

Labour of love

Work undertaken for the pleasure of doing it without hope of payment.

Usage– Ganesh's paintings were his *labour of love* and he never meant to put them up for sale.

Lady love

Sweetheart or beloved.

Usage– Maninder's *lady love* pushed him to play cricket professionally.

Lady of easy virtue

A prostitute.

Usage– Mark has fallen in love with a *lady of easy virtue.*

Land of the living

Present life.

Usage– Teacher asked Shamit to stop daydreaming and come back to the *land of the living*.

Land slide

A crushing defeat or victory in elections.

Usage– Rajpal enjoyed a *land slide* victory in the last elections.

Lantern of the dead

A lighted tower in a graveyard.

Usage– Indian philosophy and religion is no longer a lamp of the living but a *lantern of the dead.*

Larger than life

Excessive or exaggerated.

Usage– Vijay Mallya has a *larger than life* image of someone who lives life on his own terms.

Last straw

Beyond which there can be no endurance.

Usage– This budget may be the *last straw* that the Indian public needs to vote this government out of office.

Laughing stock

To be scorned at.

Usage– Her weird haircut has made her the *laughing stock* of the school.

Laughter is the best medicine

Literal.

Usage– The doctor asked the cancer patient to stay as cheerful and upbeat as possible, saying that *laughter is the best medicine.*

Lead someone up the garden path

To deceive or give false information.

Usage– The director *led the nubile girl up the garden path* by promising her a role in his movie.

Lead with the chin

To speak or behave without fear of consequences.

Usage– A good leader needs to *lead with the chin.*

Leaf out of one's book

To learn a lesson from somebody.

Usage– Those who fear oppressive dictatorship should *take a leaf out of the book* of our freedom fighters.

Left hand does not know what the right hand is doing

Lack of communication.

Usage– It is difficult to work for the progress of the company if the *left hand does not know what the right hand is doing.*

Left in the dark

Not to be given the information one wants.

Usage– She told the doctor that she did not want to be *left in the dark* about her line of treatment.

Left to one's own devices

To be able to do what one wants.

Usage– Aditya turned the whole house upside down when his mother *left him to his own devices.*

Lend an ear

To hear.

Usage– The speaker asked the audience to *lend him an ear.*

Leopard cannot change its spots

People cannot change their innate nature

Usage– Anil continues with his philandering ways despite being married; after all, a *leopard cannot change its spots.*

Let be

Leave undisturbed.

Usage– I asked the girl to *let the dog be.*

Let bygones be bygones

To forget the past.

Usage– The friends decided to let *bygones be bygones.*

Let not the sun go down on your wrath

Do not hold on to your anger for more than a day

Usage– Though Shristi was hurt by her friend's behavior, she decided to not *let the sun go down on her wrath* and called her up to clear the air.

Let sleeping dogs lie

Not to disturb an existing situation.

Usage– When Anand wanted to reopen the case against the corrupt police official, his lawyer advised him to *let sleeping dogs lie.*

Let the cat out of the bag

To disclose secrets.

Usage– The nurse *let the cat out of the bag* when she told Jaya's mother that she was pregnant.

Let the grass grow under your feet

To delay taking action.

Usage– Swaroop *let the grass grow under his feet* and did not apply for the job when there was a vacancy.

Let your hair down

To relax and not be inhibited.

Usage– Arshad wanted Dia to *let her hair down* and chill at the party.

Level best

One's utmost.

Usage– He did his *level best* to pacify the two friends.

Liberty hall

A place where one may do what one pleases.

Usage– The professor told the ruffian, "This is a university, not *Liberty Hall.*"

Lick one's boots

Sycophants.

Usage– Those who *lick your boots* when they want favors are the ones who stab your back when they get them.

Lie at one's door

To be directly responsible.

Usage– The reason for Sumer's arrogance and conceit *lies at his rich father's door.*

Lie low

Keep out of sight; bide one's time

Usage– After some Muslim terrorists blew up a bus full of tourists, the Muslims residing in the area decided to *lie low* till matters settled down.

Life begins at forty

Best part of life is the middle age.

Usage– Cherie is a living example of the fact that *life begins at forty.*

Life is just a bowl of cherries

Life is simple and pleasant.

Usage– Boman is a rich man's son and his *life is just a bowl of cherries.*

Light at the end of the tunnel

Signs of hope in the future.

Usage– The pregnancy positive report signaled *light at the end of the tunnel* for the couple undergoing IVF.

Light years ahead

A long way.

Usage– America is *light years ahead* of India in terms of employment opportunities and career growth potential.

Like a bat out of hell

Extremely quickly.

Usage– Genelia was out of the class *like a bat out of hell* as soon as the bell rang.

Like a bear with a sore head

In a foul or complaining mood.

Usage– Her husband acts *like a bear with a sore head* when he doesn't get his way.

Like a cat on a hot tin roof

Nervous or excited.

Usage– She behaved *like a cat on a hot tin roof* just before her exams.

Like a duck to water

To have a natural talent for something.

Usage– My daughter is a natural dancer and has taken to dancing *like a duck to water.*

Like a fish out of water

Uncomfortable.

Usage– Dhruv felt *like a fish out of water* at the doctors' conference.

Like a headless chicken

Directionless and aimless.

Usage– The kid ran about *like a headless chicken* in the toy store.

Like a kid in candy store

Literal.

Usage– Bhuj was *like a kid in a candy store* when he entered the pub for the first time in his life.

Like a moth to a flame
Irresistibly and dangerously drawn to someone or something
Usage– Vikrant liked adventure, and was drawn to dangerous sports *like a moth to a flame.*

Like father, like son
Literal.
Usage– When Michael's son won the golf championship, his friends congratulated him, saying *like father, like son.*

Like peas in pod
Identical.
Usage– You cannot tell the twins apart, they are *like peas in a pod.*

Like the back of your hand
To know something well.
Usage– I know the lanes and by lanes of Ajmer *like the back of my hand.*

Line of battle
Arrangement in line to meet the enemy.
Usage– The warring neighbors had drawn their *line of battle.*

Lion's share
The greater part.
Usage– My sister got the *lion's share* of our ancestral property.

Lions led by donkeys
Literal, used for British soldiers during World War I
Usage – The class of '85 had very intelligent students, but the teachers were not inspiring enough; it was a case of *lions being led by donkeys.*

Lip service
Insincere words.
Usage– The minister was capable of providing only *lip service* and nothing more.

Little strokes fell great oaks

Literal.

Usage– Mother wanted me to do my project on my own by breaking it down in little steps. *Little strokes fell great oaks,* she said.

Live and let live

Give and expect tolerance.

Usage– The principle of *'live and let live'* is important for harmonious coexistence.

Lock, stock barrel

The whole; altogether.

Usage– The British finally left India *lock, stock and barrel* in 1947.

Long shot

A bet with small chance of success.

Usage– Although the new candidate seemed like a *long shot,* the party still decided to back him.

Look after the pennies and the pounds will look after themselves

Literal.

Usage– Sarkar believed in spending wisely, saying that if you *look after the pennies and the pounds will look after themselves.*

Look before you leap

Be sure of what is ahead of you before making a decision that cannot be reversed

Usage– When Avinash told his mother that he wanted to marry Paroma, she said, "Son, be careful, *look before you leap.*"

Look daggers

Look angrily.

Usage– Neha *looked daggers* at the eve teaser.

Look down on
To despise.
Usage– One should not *look down on* the poor.

Look into
To inspect closely; to investigate.
Usage– Please *look into* the matter at the earliest.

Look like a million dollars
Literal.
Usage– Zenia *looks like a million dollars* after losing weight.

Look upto
Respect.
Usage– Students should always *look up to* their teachers.

Loose cannon
Unpredictable; difficult to control.
Usage– The young teenage brothers were like *loose cannon* and their parents had a tough time trying to discipline them.

Loose ends
Literal.
Usage– The police officer wanted to tie all the *loose ends* of the case before submitting his report.

Loose lips sink ship
Big mouth.
Usage– I asked her not to divulge more information to her fiancé than was needed, because *loose lips sink ships.*

Lose face
Be humiliated; lose reputation
Usage– Shraddha did not want to *lose face* in front of her friends, so she put on a brave face and stuck by her unfaithful husband's side.

Lose oneself

To lose one's way; to become bewildered or rapt.

Usage– Please don't *lose yourself* in the crowd.

Lose one's nerve

Lose courage.

Usage– By the time it was Vandana's turn for paragliding, she *lost her nerve* and cancelled it.

Lose your marbles

Go mad.

Usage– She seems to have *lost her marbles.*

Lower than a snake's belly

Of low moral standing.

Usage– His character is *lower than a snake's belly* and he won't think twice before betraying his best friend.

Luck of the devil

Lucky person.

Usage– Hugh has the *luck of the devil* – everything that he touches turns to gold.

•••

M

Mad as a March hare

Completely mad

Usage– Kylon behaved *mad as a March hare* after getting drunk.

Mad as a wet hen

Very angry.

Usage– The kid's mother became *mad as a wet hen* when she learnt that the teacher had slapped her son.

Made to order

Made as desired.

Usage– He wanted to wear *made to order* suits from Saville Row.

Maid of honor

A lady in the service of a Queen, a princess or a rich lady.

Usage– Gwen had been the Queen's *maid of honor* for over a decade.

Maiden battle

First contest.

Usage– The warrior was quite apprehensive about his *maiden battle.*

Maiden speech

One's first speech.

Usage– He got a standing ovation for his *maiden speech* in the college club.

Make amends

To compensate.

Usage– The teacher advised Alan to *make amends* for his misbehavior with his friend.

Make a clean breast of

Make a full disclosure; to confess

Usage– Hanif decided to *make a clean breast of* things and confess his crime to the police.

Make good

Mend.

Usage– When Ishika lost her brother's books, she promised to *make good* his loss.

Make Hay

To make the most of.

Usage– The class decided to *make hay* when the teacher was away.

Make head nor tail

Unable to find any sense in it.

Usage– I can *make* neither *head nor tail* of your letter.

Make light of

To give no importance.

Usage– Sheila *made light of* my troubles.

Make merry

To enjoy.

Usage– The friends decided to get together and *make merry* on the last day of school.

Make my day

To brighten up my day

Usage – My teacher's compliment *made my day.*

Make one's bed and lie in it

Be responsible for one's actions.

Usage– When Saroj was getting nervous for her result, her father told her that she had *made her bed, now she must lie in it.*

Make one's hair stand on end

Something frightening

Usage– A loud noise and a moving shadow in the middle of the night made Hari's *hair stand on end.*

Make one's mouth water

Literal.

Usage– The flavor of the chicken curry *made my mouth water.*

Make or mar

To cause success or ruin.

Usage– The interview can *make or mar* his career prospects.

Make out
Decipher; to understand.
Usage– I am trying to *make out* what the drawings mean.

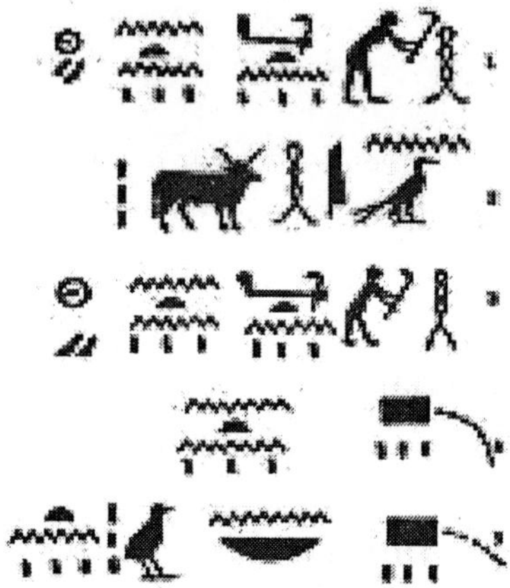

Make over
Reconstruct.
Usage– Vibha looked stylish after her *makeover.*

Make up
Fabricate; to repair; to use paint and powder on face.
Usage– Her *make up* looked shoddy.

Make your blood boil
Make you very angry.
Usage– It *made my blood boil* to see the old man hitting the small boy with a stick.

Make your skin crawl
To feel revolted or repulsed.
Usage– The leper's open sores *made my skin crawl.*

Make your hair stand on end

To be terrified.

Usage– The horror movie *made my hair stand on end.*

Make yourself scarce

To go away.

Usage– When I saw the mob becoming angry, I decided to *make myself scarce.*

Man after my own heart

A kindred spirit; someone I agree with

Usage– Jason is honest and sincere – a *man after my own heart.*

Man does not live by bread alone

Man needs spiritual nourishment as much as he needs physical nourishment

Usage– Jeet was not happy working for the corrupt boss; after all, *man does not live by bread alone.*

Man friday

An assistant or odd job attendant.

Usage– He feels handicapped without his *Man Friday.*

Man of his word

One who keeps his promise.

Usage– Bhishma was a *man of his word.*

Man of letters

A scholar.

Usage– The professor was a *man of letters.*

Man of means

Wealthy.

Usage– Satish is a *man of means.*

Man's best friend

Dogs.

Usage– More than books, she relies on *man's best friend* to give her company.

Man's man

A man who does and enjoys things which other men enjoy.

Usage– Joseph is a *man's man* and enjoys adventure sports above everything else.

Many a slip twixt the cup and the lip

Literal.

Usage– Cheryl's project derailed in the last stage; there's *many a slip twixt the cup and the lip.*

Many a true word is spoken in jest

Truth is found in comic utterances

Usage– Deepak camouflages his suggestions to his employees in jokes; *many a true word is spoken in jest.*

Many moons ago

A long time ago.

Usage– We had gone on an African safari *many moons ago.*

Marching orders

Order to march.

Usage– The junior clerk received his *marching orders* from the boss.

Marry in haste, repent at leisure

Literal

Usage– The star's whirlwind romance followed by a fairytale wedding led to divorce in no time at all. *Marry in haste, repent at leisure.*

Matter of course

A thing occurring in natural order and time.

Usage– Seed becomes a fruit as a *matter of course.*

Matter of life and death

Very important.

Usage– Getting the coveted role became a *matter of life and death* for the star.

Meet half way

Give concessions in compromise.

Usage– Father offered to *meet me half way* by offering to foot my telephone bills.

Meet your match

Someone as good, if not better, than you.

Usage– When Sharanya defeated me in tennis, I knew I had *met my match.*

Melt one's heart

Cause pity.

Usage– The sight of small children begging for alms *melts the heart* of even the most hard hearted.

Memory like an elephant

Very good memory.

Usage– My mother has *memory like an elephant* and remembers all dates and numbers by heart.

Mend fences

Mend relationships.

Usage– 'Aman ki Asha' is an endeavor to *mend fences* between India and Pakistan.

Mend one's ways

Reform one's behavior.

Usage– You ought to *mend your ways* if you want to be successful.

Merchant prince

A merchant of great wealth and power.

Usage– Soniya's father was a *merchant prince* in Kuwait.

Middle of the road

Take a moderate stand; not opting for either extremes

Usage– Buddha preached taking the *middle of the road* in order to avoid suffering and unhappiness.

Milk of human kindness

Natural kindness.

Usage– Mother Teresa's face dripped with the *milk of human kindness*.

Millstone round your neck

A problem which prevents you from doing what you want.

Usage– Her little baby was like a *millstone round her neck* and made it impossible for her to travel for work.

Mind your P's and Q's
To be watchfully accurate and punctilious.

Usage– You must *mind your P's and Q's* when you are dealing with an important dignitary.

Mind's eye
Visual imagination; mental view.

Usage– The poet could see the beautiful daffodils in his *mind's eye*.

Misery acquaints a man with strange bedfellows
Literal

Usage– Amandeep realized that *misery acquaints a man with strange bedfellows* when his neighbor turned out to be a pillar of support for him during his income tax raid.

Money doesn't grow on trees
Money is not earned easily.

Usage– When I asked my father for a new car, he said, "*Money doesn't grow on trees*, son, work hard and earn for it yourself."

Money to burn
Someone who is very rich.

Usage– Her daughter gifted her a smart Louis Vuitton handbag. Oh well, they have a lot of *money to burn*.

Monkey tricks/business
Deceitful action.

Usage– His mother told him that his *monkey tricks* would land the whole family into trouble.

More and more
Continually increasing.

Usage– Television's influence is increasing *more and more* everyday.

More holes then Swiss cheese

Incomplete.

Usage– The witness' story had *more holes than Swiss cheese.*

More than meets the eye

More complex than it appears.

Usage– The bruises on her face don't look like she's had a fall; there's *more than meets the eye.*

More than one way to skin a cat

There are different ways of doing the same thing.

Usage– When Hanif's father refused to give him permission to go to the party, Hanif started thinking of alternate ways. After all, there is *more than one way to skin a cat.*

Mortal hurry

In great hurry.

Usage– Radhika was in *mortal hurry* to reach the station on time.

Mother earth

Earth as mother of its inhabitants.

Usage– My teacher tells us to respect *mother earth.*

Mother tongue

One's native tongue.

Usage– Barbara's *mother tongue* is Spanish.

Move heavem and warth

To make strenuous efforts.

Usage– The boy *moved heaven and earth* to get the job.

Move mountains

Make every effort.

Usage– Zidane was willing to *move mountains* to get admission in a college of his choice.

Mover and shaker

An influential and important person.

Usage– All the *movers and shakers* of the industry were present at the glitzy wedding.

Much ado about nothing

To exaggerate a trifling matter.

Usage– Haider's fuss about his dog's ill health was really *much ado about nothing.*

Much of a muchness

Similar; difficult to distinguish

Usage– The homework of the two friends had too *much of a muchness* to be ignored.

Mud slinging

Make unworthy charges.

Usage– The *mud slinging* between the friends made the whole scene very ugly.

Muddle through

To blunder through difficult situations.

Usage– He *muddle through* his new job for the first few months.

Mumbo jumbo

Nonsense; spurious religious ritual

Usage– The man felt frightened by the meaningless *mumbo jumbo* of the priest's chants.

Mum's the word

To remain silent.

Usage– When my mother asked me something personal about my friend, I told her *mum's the word.*

Mutton dressed as lamb

Middle aged people trying to look younger.

Usage– When Rosy came to my house wearing her daughter's clothes, I could hear snide references to *mutton dressed as lamb.*

My heart bleeds

Feel sympathy and sadness.

Usage– *My heart bleeds* for the poor homeless orphans begging on the streets.

My heart goes out

Feel sympathy for.

Usage– *My heart goes out* to the poor boy who lost the first position by half a mark.

•••

N

Nail in the coffin

An action which eventually would lead to a problem.

Usage– By lying to his boss time and again, Biren was driving a *nail in his coffin*.

Namby pamby

Colorless; sentimental; childish.

Usage– Sania's boyfriend is a *namby pamby* young man.

Neck and neck

Very close.

Usage– The two leaders were *neck and neck* in the polls.

Necessity is the mother of invention

Difficulties inspire clever solutions

Usage– I saw a grocery vendor with a motorized contraption of his pushcart and I thought to myself, '*Necessity is the mother of invention.*'

Necessity knows no law

Literal.

Usage– The thief told the judge that stealing was a necessity for him, and *necessity knows no law.*

Need and necessity

Vitally important.

Usage– Integrated education is the *need and necessity* of today's life.

Needle in a haystack

To engage in a hopeless search.

Usage– Divya knew that trying to find her little poodle in the busy metropolitan was like looking for a *needle in haystack.*

Ne'er do well

Good for nothing.

Usage– Joshua was a *ne'erdo well* and his parents had no expectations from him.

Neither a borrower nor a lender be

Literal

Usage– When Arman asked Nikhil for a loan, he told him, "I follow the age old wisdom of the saying – *neither a borrower nor a lender be."*

Neither here nor there

Of very little importance.

Usage– Shakira likes to play the piano, but that's *neither here nor there* since her parents want her to become a doctor.

Nerves of steels

Strong and courageous.

Usage– Soldiers have to possess *nerves of steel.*

Nest egg

Savings.

Usage– The wise businessman had put aside a *nest egg* for the rainy day.

Nether world

Hell.

Usage– The movie showed gruesome scenes about creatures living in the *nether world.*

Never too late to mend

One can improve matters at any stage.

Usage– The marriage counselor told the couple that it was *never too late to mend.*

Never look a gift horse in the mouth

Don't be ungrateful when you receive a gift

Usage– When Arpita enquired about the price of the cardigan she had received as a gift, her mother admonished her and said, *"Never look a gift horse in the mouth."*

New blood

Young and fresh people.

Usage– Our political scenario needs *new blood.*

New brush sweeps clean

A new person sees things from a fresh perspective.

Usage– My mother in law told me that my ideas of running the household may be fresh but she had the experience; *a new brush sweeps clean*, but the old one knows the corners.

New kid on the block

Literal.

Usage– When I joined the newspaper and was the *new kid on the block* I had to run errands for the other staff members.

Next of kin

Nearest relative.

Usage– My daughter is my *next of kin.*

Nigger in the wood pile

A hidden motive; a secret betrayer.

Usage– When the minister went out of the way to grant a favor, I was sure there was a *nigger in the wood pile.*

Nine day's wonder

Shortlived sensation.

Usage– The starlet was happy to be a *nine day's wonder.*

Ninteen to the dozen

With great volubility.

Usage– The young man talked *nineteen to the dozen.*

Nine times out of ten

Chances are far greater.

Usage– *Nine times out of ten* his prediction about the share price is correct.

Nip and tuck

A close contest where neither opponent seems to be gaining.

Usage– They ran *nip and tuck* to reach the destination.

Nip in the bud

Cut off in the earliest stage.

Usage– Evil must be *nipped in the bud.*

Nitty gritty

Basic essentials; harsh realities; heart of the matter

Usage– The shrewd businessman cut down the frivolous banter and got down to the *nitty gritty* of the project under consideration.

No great shakes

Not very good at something.

Usage– Farhad may brag about it, but he is *no great shakes* as a golf player.

No holds barred

To be able to do anything.

Usage– The friends had a *no holds barred* conversation.

No man is an island

Literal

Usage – Theresa enjoyed the priest's sermon on the common brotherhood of man where he said that *no man is an island* and we are all a part of the bigger picture.

No man's land

A waste land on which no one has a recognized claim; a debatable land between entrenched hostile forces.

Usage– I was born in the *no man's land* between India and Nepal.

No questions asked

Literal.

Usage– The chief had implicit faith in his foreman, and *no questions asked.*

No skin off my nose

Not be affected or bothered.

Usage– When my driver left without any notice it was *no skin off my nose* since I knew driving.

No spine

Cowardly.

Usage– Junaid has *no spine* and cannot stand up to his father.

No time to lose

Literal.

Usage– Since Santosh started studying quite late, he realized that he had *no time to lose.*

No use to man or beast

Utterly useless.

Usage– The old washing machine had to be sold to the scrap dealer since it was *no use to man or beast.*

Nodding acquaitance

Slight acquaintance as with a person one nods but does not speak to.

Usage– Preeti is my morning walk's *nodding acquaintance.*

None so blind as those who will not see

Literal.

Usage– Hazel did not believe me when I told her that her brother was taking drugs. Really, there is *none so blind as those who will not see.*

Nook and corner

Everywhere.

Usage– I looked for him in every *nook and corner.*

Nosey parker

Inquisitive; prying

Usage– Mrs. Wilson is a *nosey parker* and the neighbor's are tired of her prying and snooping.

Not all there

A little stupid or crazy.

Usage– His grandmother is *not all there,* so don't take her words seriously.

Not have the heart

Not have the strength or courage to do something.

Usage– She did *not have the heart* to tell her brother that he had failed.

Not my cup of tea

Not to like something.

Usage– Aerobics is *not my cup of tea.*

Not the only pebble on the beach

There are other alternatives.

Usage– When Sidhesh turned down the marriage proposal, Aradhna was not worried since he is *not the only pebble on the beach.*

Nothing is certain but death and taxes

Literal

Usage – When Anuradha asked her plumber if he was certain that the leak in her roof had been plugged, he smiled, *"Nothing is certain but death and taxes."*

Nothing ventured, nothing gained

One can't win if one doesn't play.

Usage– One has to take certain risks in business, because *nothing ventured, nothing gained.*

Nothing succeeds like success

Success breeds further success

Usage– On getting out of rehab, Brinda picked up a job and has already been promoted twice; *nothing succeeds like success.*

Now and again

Sometimes; from time to time.

Usage– He goes to Switzerland *now and again.*

Nuts and bolts

Most essential components.

Usage– The staff is like *nuts and bolts,* and each one contributes to the smooth functioning of the whole machinery.

•••

O

Occupational disease/hazard

A disease common among workers engaged in a particular occupation.

Usage– Exposure to chemicals is an *occupational hazard* of the scientists.

Odds and ends

Remnants; small odd articles.

Usage– She makes handicraft items with *odds and ends* of wood.

Off and on

Now and then.

Usage– He comes to see me *off and on*.

Off color

Look ill.

Usage– Vidya looked *off color* today.

Off the beaten track

Not the usual path.

Usage– Karan's choice of career may be *off the beaten track*, but he is earning well.

Off the hook

Out of trouble.

Usage– The lawyer got Viren *off the hook.*

Off the record

Something said in confidence

Usage– The star told the reporter, "This conversation is *off the record.*"

Off your rocker

Crazy, silly.

Usage– He must be *off his rocker* to turn down this proposal.

Oil the wheels

Make things go smoothly.

Usage– For success in professional life, one has to *oil the wheels* with courtesy and discipline.

Old flame

Someone one has been in love with.

Usage– Aamir ran into his *old flame* at the supermarket.

Old friends and old wine are best

Literal.

Usage– Some things need to stand the test of time; that's why *old friends and old wine are best.*

Old head on young shoulders
Wisdom beyond years.
Usage– Siddharth has an *old head on young shoulders* and maturity beyond his years.

Old maid
Spinster.
Usage– Robin's aunt is an *old maid* and keeps house for him.

Old wives' tale
A proverb or piece of advice.
Usage– There is age old wisdom in some *old wives' tale* even if they are not backed by scientific evidence.

Olive branch
A symbol of peace.
Usage– The Sharmas held out the *olive branch* to the Iyengars to end the cold war by inviting them over.

On a fishing expedition
Try to get information indirectly.
Usage– Suri was off *on a fishing expedition* with my driver to find out all about my trip.

On a silver platter
To get something too easily.
Usage– Being the CEO's son got him the job *on a silver platter*.

On all fours

Crawling.

Usage– Veena got down *on all fours* to clean the corner under the bed.

On hold

No action being taken.

Usage– The school principal decided to put the decision *on hold* till he'd heard the student's side of the story.

On the case

Some one who is dealing with the issue on hand.

Usage– Though the friends have still not patched up, I am *on the case.*

On the dot

Punctually.

Usage– She arrived at seven *on the dot.*

On the house

Get something for free.

Usage– The new groom announced that all the drinks that evening would be *on the house.*

On the line

At risk.

Usage– Vaishnavi's job is *on the line* after her boss caught her napping on the job.

On the map

A place which becomes widely known.

Usage– Movies and advertisements have put Koh Samui *on the map* as the ideal tourist destination.

On the same page

Someone who is thinking the same way.

Usage– Abhijeet was glad that his parents were *on the same page* where his matrimonial plans were concerned.

On the same wavelength

To have same ideas and opinions.

Usage– I enjoy Avneesh's company because we are *on the same wavelength.*

On the tip of your tongue

Literal.

Usage– The woman's name was *on the tip of my tongue* but I could not remember it.

On the up and up

Making good progress.

Usage– Srinath's business is *on the up and up* nowadays.

On top of the world

Feeling great and doing well.

Usage– Trishala is *on top of the world* these days after scoring so well in her exams.

On the warpath

Confrontation; fight

Usage– The two friends have been *on the warpath* for the last couple of months now.

On your toes

Alert and ready to go.

Usage– My little baby keeps me *on my toes.*

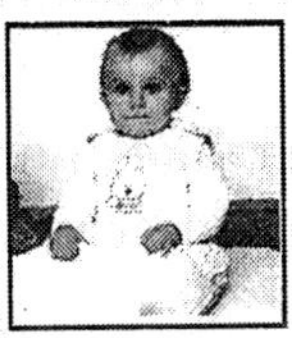

Once and for all

Forever.

Usage– Let us come to an agreement about our divorce *once and for all.*

Once in a blue moon

Rarely

Usage– Ramanna doesn't enjoy socializing and meets his friends *once in a blue moon.*

One bad apple

One wrong person, idea or action can ruin everything around.

Usage– Vandy was the *bad apple* who was responsible for the split between the friends.

One for the road

The last drink for the day.

Usage– Srichand decided that he would take *one for the road* and leave the pub.

One good turn deserves another

Literal.

Usage– When my colleague asked me to help her with a project, I promised I would do it if she came out for coffee with me. After all, *one good turn deserves another.*

One man's meat is another man's poison / one man's trash is another man's treasure

Literal.

Usage– Dilshad neither likes nor understands cricket, whereas her husband is addicted to it; *one man's meat is another man's poison.*

One swallow does not make a summer

One good event does not mean that everything is all right.

Usage– Though her mother's first blood test report is normal, the family is awaiting the results of the second one; after all, *one swallow does not make a summer.*

Open book

Transparent.

Usage– The little girl's face was like an *open book.*

Open old sores

Reopen old issues or enmity.

Usage– When Raghu met Vatsala for the first time after their divorce, he *opened old sores* all over again.

Open letter

A letter addressed to a person but intended for public reading.

Usage– I enjoyed reading Jawahar Lal Nehru's *open letter* to his daughter, Indira Gandhi.

Open mind

An unprejudiced mind.

Usage– He has got an *open mind.*

Open season

A time when criticism and negative reactions are to be expected

Usage – After the President's callous response to the Naxalite massacre, his PRO knew that it would be *open season* for the media.

Open secret

A matter known to many.

Usage– Corruption in the highest political circle is an *open secret*.

Order of battle

Order of troops, ships, aero planes etc. in readiness for war.

Usage– The party high command are chalking out the *order of battle* for the coming elections.

Original sin

The sin of Adam.

Usage– Bible talks about Adam, Eve and the *original sin*.

Out and out

Completely.

Usage– He is an *out and out* womanizer.

Out of character

Not in keeping with character.

Usage– Screaming at the servants was *out of character* for the gentle Mary.

Out of favor

Disliked.

Usage– I found myself *out of favor* with my friend when I did not flatter him.

Out of hand
Beyond control.
Usage– The riot situation got *out of hand* and the army had to be called to restore peace.

Out of print
No longer in print by the publisher.
Usage– I was looking for an old book which had been *out of print* for a number of years.

Out of sight out of mind
Literal.
Usage– When we moved town, I slowly lost touch with my friends; it was a case of *out of sight and out of mind.*

Out of sorts
Mildly unwell
Usage– Jatin looked *out of sorts,* so his boss asked him to take the day off.

Out of the blue
Suddenly and unexpectedly.
Usage– The job offer came *out of the blue.*

Out of the mouths of babes and sucklings
Literal
Usage– When my little daughter comforted me with wise words, I was amazed to hear such judicious advice *out of the mouths of babes and sucklings.*

Over and above
In addition.
Usage– He informed us about the extra charges *over and above* the MRP.

Over and over

Many times; repeatedly.

Usage– I wanted to read the old classic *over and over.*

Over my dead body

To not let something happen.

Usage– Justin told his son that he could get an ear piercing done only *over his dead body.*

Over the hill

Of mature age.

Usage– Anjuman did not get the job as the management thought he was *over the hill.*

Over the moon

Overjoyed.

Usage– The child was *over the moon* when I gave him an ice cream.

Over the top

Excessive or unnecessary.

Usage– Rosy went *over the top* with her accessory matching.

Own up

Confess.

Usage– The criminal decided to *own up* his offences.

•••

P

Pack of fools

A group of idiots.

Usage– Mohan did not like to mix with his classmates and considered them to be just a *pack of fools.*

Pack off

To send off quickly.

Usage– She *packed off* the dishonest servant.

Packed like sardines

Extremely crowded.

Usage– The railway compartment had people *packed like sardines.*

Paddle your own canoe

Do things for oneself.

Usage–Nikhil refused his father's help to set up his business because he wanted to *paddle his own canoe.*

Pain in the neck

Annoying and irritating.

Usage– Hiten's mother is a *pain in the neck.*

Paint the lily

To attempt to beautify that which is already beautiful.

Usage– When Rakhi was applying make up, her husband told her that she was *painting the lily*.

Paint the town red

To enjoy a boisterous spree.

Usage– After the exams, the students decided to go out and *paint the town red*.

Pain someone black

To criticize or malign a person.

Usage– Manmohan *painted his friend black* when he refused to lend him money.

Pale hearted

Dispirited.

Usage– After losing his job, Shetty has now become *palehearted*.

Paper tiger

Something or someone who only looks powerful.

Usage– Harpreet's father is a *paper tiger*, actually it's his mother who rules the roost.

Paradise on earth

A living heaven.

Usage– The photographs of the lazy backwaters of Kerala make it look like *paradise on earth*.

Part and parcel

An essential part.

Usage– Patience and persuasion are *part and parcel* of a salesman's job profile.

Pass away

To come to an end; die.

Usage– Bedi's mother *passed away* after a long illness.

Pass off

Impostor, to act fraudulently.

Usage– He could easily *pass off* for a minister.

Pass out

To faint; dead drunk.

Usage– Tanmay was drinking heavily all evening, and he *passed out* on the dance floor.

Pass over

To overlook; to ignore.

Usage– Omar was very dejected when he was *passed over* for promotion.

Pass the buck

Evade responsibility by passing it on to someone else

Usage– When the teacher asked whose idea it was to bunk the classes, Suri *passed the buck* to Cherie.

Pass the time of the day

Literal.

Usage– Old men like to *pass the time of day* in a garden.

Pass through

Experience; undergo.

Usage– My brother *passed through* many hardships before settling down in his career.

Passage of arms

Quarrel of words.

Usage– The new session of the Parliament saw a *passage of arms* between the prominent leaders.

Passive resistance

Deliberate refusal to do what law orders using peaceful means.

Usage– Mahatma Gandhi pioneered the principle of *passive resistance* in India.

Pat on the back

A mark of encouragement or approval.

Usage– The professor gave Jahnavi a *pat on the back.*

Patience of Job

Great patience, as exemplified by a Biblical character, Job.

Usage– Celina has the *patience of Job* with her children.

Pave the way for

To prepare the way for; make easier.

Usage– His brother's job *paved the way* for his placement in the big company.

Pay through the nose

Pay heavily.

Usage– He *paid through the nose* for his wife's birthday dress.

Pay one back in one's own coin/tit for tat.

Usage– When Caroline cheated on her husband, he wanted to *pay her back in the same coin.*

Peeping Tom
A sly peeper.
Usage– Sophie's new neighbor is a *peeping Tom.*

Pen is mightier than the sword
Literal.
Usage– The journalist asked the industrialist not to threaten him because the *pen is mightier than the sword.*

Penny for your thoughts
Said to someone who appears thoughtful.
Usage– "Here's a *penny for your thoughts,*" said my friend when I didn't hear him the second time.

Penny wise pound foolish
Someone who is careful with small amounts of money, but not large sums.
Usage– Lucy is *penny wise pound foolish* and doesn't pay attention to minor repairs around her house.

Pepper and salt
Mingled black and white.
Usage– He looks great with *pepper and salt* hair.

Perish the thought
Literal.
Usage– When my son wanted a new car, I told him, "*Perish the thought,* it won't ever happen."

Pet aversion
Chief object of dislike.
Usage– Flattery is his *pet aversion.*

Petty cash

Small sum of money.

Usage– The accountant was caught swindling the *petty cash.*

Photo finish

A neck to neck finish of any contest.

Usage– The *photo finish* at the end of the Derby made it so much more thrilling.

Pick a hole in one's coat

To find fault with.

Usage– He has the habit of *picking holes in his friend's coats.*

Pick and choose

Select fastidiously.

Usage– My father took his time to *pick and choose* the right man for all his daughters.

Pick me up

A stimulating drink.

Usage– Dharmesh wanted a *pick me up* before his guests arrived.

Pick a quarrel

To seek a fight.

Usage– Harsh avoids *picking a quarrel* with anyone.

Pick one's pocket

To steal from someone's pocket.

Usage– The thief made an unsuccessful attempt to *pick my pocket.*

Piece of cake

Really easy.

Usage– Preparing a sumptuous four course meal is a *piece of cake* for Madhubala.

Piece of one's mind
A frank and outspoken opinion.
Usage– When Rachit tried to misbehave with me, I gave him a *piece of my mind.*

Piece by piece
Little by little.
Usage– He dismantled the bed, *piece by piece.*

Piece together
Put together bit by bit.
Usage– The detective *pieced together* bits of evidence to find out the truth.

Pig headed
Stupid.
Usage– Do not talk to that man; he is simply *pig-headed.*

Pig in a poke
Buy undesirable things without examining them.
Usage– Mother asked me to be careful and not buy *pig in a poke.*

Pigs might fly
Wonders might happen.
Usage– Piyush might get through his exams, and *pigs might fly.*

Pin one's faith on
To put entire trust in.
Usage– He advised his brother to *pin his faith on* God and hope for the best.

Pins and needles
A tingling feeling; prickly feel.
Usage– Politics bequeaths a crown of *pins and needles.*

Pinch of salt

With some caution.

Usage– Arjun tends to exaggerate, so I take his words with a *pinch of salt*.

Pipe down

Subside into silence.

Usage– The critics *piped down* after hearing the writer's fiery speech.

Piping hot

Extremely hot.

Usage– I love my coffee *piping hot*.

Pitter patter

With light pattering sound.

Usage– Rain fell *pitter patter* on the window sill.

Plain as a pikestaff

Quite clear.

Usage– The animosity between the two friends was *plain as a pikestaff*.

Plain sailing

Smooth or easy going.

Usage– Once he got the work permit, it was all *plain sailing* for him.

Plan B

An alternate or fall back plan.

Usage– The army had to fall back on *Plan B* when the original plan of action failed.

Play at

Engage in the game of; make pretence of.

Usage– When the girl started flirting with Jignesh, he thought to himself that this was a game two could *play at.*

Play fast and loose

To act in an inconsistent and reckless fashion.

Usage– David is playing *fast and loose* with his girlfriend.

Play havoc

Creating disorder and confusion.

Usage– Computer virus *played havoc* with my files.

Play into someone's hands

To do what someone wants you to do.

Usage– The masses *played into the wily politician's hands* and broke into the mosque.

Play one's cards well

Make a good use of opportunities.

Usage– The criminal's wife *played her cards well,* and got compensation from the government on sympathy grounds.

Play second fiddle

Take on a small or junior's role.

Usage– She was not happy *playing second fiddle* to her rich and powerful husband.

Play the fool

To act like a fool.

Usage– The boss asked him not to *play the fool* and take his work seriously.

Play the man

To act bravely.

Usage– The little boy tried to *play the man* by not showing how upset he was.

Plead guilty

Admit guilt.

Usage– The culprit *pleaded guilty* to all the charges.

Pleased as punch

Satisfied and content.

Usage– He was *pleased as punch* about getting his new car.

Please yourself

Do as you like.

Usage– If you don't want to do what I say, *please yourself.*

Plough the sands

Work in vain, unfruitful venture.

Usage– Farhad's work made him feel that he was trying to *plough the sands.*

Pluck up

To summon courage; to gather strength.

Usage– Manish *plucked up* courage to tell his feelings to Asha.

Poetic justice

Just administration of reward and punishment.

Usage– The drug dealer's death by overdose of drugs was nothing short of *poetic justice.*

Poetry in motion

Beautiful to watch.

Usage– The spellbinding ballet was *poetry in motion.*

Point for point

Exactly in all particulars.

Usage– The client accepted his terms of agreement *point for point.*

Point of honor

Question of dignity.

Usage– The girl felt slighted on the *point of honor.*

Point of order

A question of rules.

Usage– He was rusticated from school on the *point of order.*

Point of view

The position from which one looks at anything.

Usage– There is a great difference in our *points of view.*

Point out

Literal.

Usage– He *pointed out* that he was not wrong in the matter.

Poison one's ears against

To set one against.

Usage– Never *poison anyone's ears against* your friends.

Poke fun at

Banter.

Usage– Please don't *poke fun at* your younger brother.

Poke one's nose

Pry.

Usage– I don't like to *poke my nose* in other people's affairs.

Polar forces

Forces that act in pairs and in different directions, as in magnetism.

Usage– The *polar forces* in international politics make its trends unpredictable and fickle.

Polish off

Finish off; dispose of.

Usage– The children *polished off* the entire bowl of pudding.

Pop off

To die; to fall asleep.

Usage– His father *popped off* last year.

Pop the question

To make an offer of marriage.

Usage– David *popped the question* to Jennifer in the party.

Port of call

Where ships can call for stores and repair.

Usage– The naval ship was expected to reach the *port of call* by midnight.

Port of entry

A port where merchandise is allowed to enter by law.

Usage– Chennai is a *port of entry*.

Pose a problem

Set a question.

Usage– Every new day *poses a new problem* for the new couple.

Pot of money

A large amount of money.

Usage– He doesn't need to work since his father has left him a *pot of money*.

Pot calling the kettle black

To criticize someone for doing something that one himself does.

Usage– When Pakistan accuses America of increasing terrorism in the world, it is clearly a case of *pot calling the kettle black.*

Pound of flesh

To force someone to pay back something which is owed.

Usage– The bank sent its off
icial to claim its *pound of flesh* from the debtor.

Pour oil on troubled waters

Try to calm things down.

Usage– The boy tried to *pour oil on troubled waters* by pacifying the aggrieved mother.

Power politics

Politics based on balance of power.

Usage– The daughters in law in the television serial play games based on *power politics.*

Powwow

To confer.

Usage– The managers *powwowed* till well past midnight.

Practical jole

A joke or annoying trick.

Usage– The boys played a *practical joke* on their teacher on the 1st of April.

Preaching to the choir

Talk about a subject on which the audience already agrees.

Usage– When his girlfriend told Nipesh that she did not want to marry in the near future, he told her she was *preaching to the choir.*

Presence of mind

Power of keeping cool and collected in emergency.

Usage– Shirish showed exemplary *presence of mind* when he locked the robbers inside the house and called the police.

Prick up one's ears

To begin to listen intently.

Usage– My son *pricks up his ears* whenever I mention a new gadget.

Primrose path

The life of pleasure.

Usage– The life of the baroness had followed the *primrose path.*

Printer's devil

Mistakes in printing.

Usage– The *printer's devil* in a cookery book could literally kill you.

Pro and con

For and against.

Usage– The professor invited the students to discuss the *pros and cons* of the topic under discussion.

Proof of the pudding is in the eating

Literal.

Usage– Rohtash envies his brother's job as the CEO of the big company, not realizing its pressures; after all, the *proof of the pudding is in the eating.*

Proud as a peacock

Very proud.

Usage– The beautiful girl was as *proud as a peacock.*

Puffed up

Swollen with pride.

Usage– His heart *puffed up* with pride when he saw his little son play football so well.

Pull a face

To grimace.

Usage– When mother told her she couldn't go to the party, she *pulled a face.*

Pull down

Demolish; reduce in health.

Usage– The building was *pulled down* to make a commercial complex.

Pull oneself together

Collect one's facultics.

Usage– Krishna implored Arjun to *pull himself together* and face the foe.

Pull soneone's leg

To joke, banter.

Usage– He asked his sister not to *pull his leg.*

Pull strings

To use contacts.

Usage– Ratan *pulled strings* to get his child admitted to the college of his choice.

Pull the wool over someone's eyes

To deceive or cheat.

Usage– The salesman *pulled the wool over his eyes* by making false claims.

Pull through

Manage to overcome a difficulty.

Usage– The family *pulled through* the period of crisis with dignity.

Pull yourself up by your boot straps

To make the effort to improve things.

Usage– Rishi *pulled himself up by his bootstraps* when he failed for the second time.

Push comes to a shove

Worst comes to worst.

Usage– If *push comes to a shove,* Jai will have to use up all his savings.

Put across

To convey.

Usage– The Prime Minister managed to *put across* the need for the bill very succinctly.

Put all your eggs in one basket

To risk everything on one opportunity.

Usage– The retired officer regretted *putting all his eggs in one basket*.

Put an end to
To cause to discontinue.
Usage– We should *put an end to* corruption.

Put by
Set aside.
Usage– Mother always asked me to *put by* something for a rainy day.

Put down
Crush; killed.
Usage– The rebellion was *put down* by the army.

Put in an appearance
Appear.
Usage– Despite differences between the two, Malti *put in an appearance* at her brother's marriage.

Put off
Postpone.
Usage– Do not *put off* till tomorrow what you can do today.

Put to death
Kill.
Usage– The killer was *put to death.*

Put to sea
Begin a voyage.
Usage– The ship was *put to sea.*

Put two and two together
Draw a conclusion from evidence.
Usage– The detectives *put two and two together* and caught the killer.

Put up with

To bear.

Usage – Bhoomi refused to *put up with* her brother's silly arguments.

Put your foot in your mouth

Say something stupid or embarrassing.

Usage – She *put her foot in her mouth* by joking about her colleague when he was within earshot.

Put your heads together

To exchange ideas.

Usage – The sales team *put their heads together* to meet the new challenges.

Put your money where your mouth is

To back up one's words with action.

Usage – Pritam *puts his money where his mouth is,* and his friends respect him for this.

•••

Q

Quail pipe
A whistle for alluring quails into a trap.
Usage– The politician won the elections with the *quail pipe* of 'More power to the masses.'

Qualms of conscience
Uneasy conscience.
Usage– The guilty suffer from *qualms of conscience* which they ignore.

Quarrel with one's bread and butter
To act in a way prejudicial to one's means of subsistence.
Usage– When Abhi fought with his boss, his brother told him it was not prudent to *quarrel with his bread and butter.*

Queen Anne is dead
That is old news.
Usage– When I told Mahesh about the neighbor's fight, he replied, "*Queen Anne is dead.*"

Queen bee
A woman who holds an important position.
Usage– Tia was the *queen bee* in her house.

Queen mother

Mother of the ruler.

Usage– The *queen mother* was the young king's guide and teacher.

Queer Street

In debt.

Usage– Throughout his life, Jeet's father lived in the *Queer Street.*

Queer the pitch

To interfere and spoil someone's chances.

Usage– Dr. Paul wants to attend to his colleague's patients and *queer the pitch* for him.

Quick as a flash

To happen very fast.

Usage– The thief disappeared *quick as a flash.*

Quick buck

Easy money.

Usage– Narender was keen to make a *quick buck.*

Quick witted

Intelligent.

Usage– Anu was the most *quick witted* boy of the class.

Quill driver

Writer.

Usage– The *quill driver* signed the contract with the leading publishing house.

Quiet as a mouse

Absolutely silent.

Usage– The children were *quiet as a mouse* when their father walked in.

•••

R

Rabid democrat
Unreasoning democrat.
Usage– Maria belongs to a family of *rabid democrats.*

Rack one's brains
Strain one's memory.
Usage– He *racked his brains* to remember her name.

Radical error
Fundamental mistake.
Usage– The mixup about the titles of the guests was a *radical error* and the secretary had to pay for it with his job.

Rag bag
A dirty untidy woman.
Usage– Rosemary's new maid is a *rag bag.*

Raid the market
Derange prices artificially for future gain.
Usage– Traders *raid the market* through monopoly purchases.

Raining cats and dogs
Raining very heavily.
Usage– When I reached the park, it was *raining cats and dogs.*

Rainy day

A possible future time of need; bad days.

Usage– You must put something by against a *rainy day.*

Raise an alarm

To give notice of danger.

Usage– When the fire broke out in the neighborhood, the people of the locality *raised an alarm.*

Raised a siege

Put an end to a siege.

Usage– If the army had not *raised the siege,* the people in the city would have starved.

Raised Cain

Make a big fuss.

Usage– The newspapers *raised Cain* about the celebrity's tactless comment.

Raised money

To get money by pawning.

Usage– She *raised money* by pawning his gold ring.

Raised one's hat

To salute.

Usage– We *raise our hat* to the freedom fighters.

Raise to bench

To become a judge.

Usage– Natwar Singh has been *raised to the bench.*

Raise from the dead

To restore to life.

Usage– When Rufus met with a terrible accident, it was his doctor who was able to *raise him from the dead.*

Rank and file
Common people.

Usage– The annual general meeting was attended by the top management as well as the *rank and file* of the company.

Rap on the knuckles
A nice beating.

Usage– The student was given a *rap on the knuckles* by the principal.

Raw deal
Harsh inequitable treatment.

Usage– The blacks received a *raw deal* in Europe in the early 19th century.

Raw youth
Inexperienced young man.

Usage– He was unhappy after appointing *raw youth* in his company.

Ray of hope
Slight hope.

Usage– The blood test report offered her a *ray of hope.*

Razor edge
A dangerous position.

Usage– Our country's economy is poised on *a razor-edge* these days.

Razzle dazzle
A rowdy frolic or spree.

Usage– The *razzle dazzle* of the wedding enchanted the little girl.

Read between the lines

To detect a meaning not expressed.

Usage– The new daughter in law was adept at *reading between the lines.*

Ready to eat

Cooked.

Usage– We packed *ready to-eat* food items for our picnic.

Ready to wear

Readymade.

Usage– She was looking for *ready-to-wear* clothes for her children.

Really and truly

Positively.

Usage– He was *really and truly* upset by the turn of events.

Reap the fruit of

To enjoy the consequences of.

Usage– The teacher told the young princes that one should sow good deeds and *reap the fruit.*

Reckon with

To call to account.

Usage– He had to *reckon with* the fact with his manager was a cheat.

Recording angel

An angel supposed to record every good and bad deed committed by a man.

Usage– I think of the *recording angel* before doing anything wrong.

Recover one's senses

To regain consciousness.

Usage– He *recovered his senses* after three days of the accident.

Red carpet

A special welcome.

Usage– The actress enjoyed walking the *red carpet* at the Cannes Festival.

Red handed

At the spot.

Usage– The manager was caught *red-handed* while taking bribe.

Red letter day

Special day

Usage– Founder's Day is a *red letter day* in the history of our school.

Red light

A danger signal; a brothel.

Usage– Father asked him not to visit the *red light* area.

Reduce to ashes

Destroyed or burnt down.

Usage– His acerbic tongue *reduced the relationship to ashes.*

Reel off

To give out with rapidity or fluency.

Usage– He *reeled off* the speech.

Rein one's anger

To control one's anger.

Usage– One must *rein one's anger* if one wants to build good relationships.

Religion is the opium of the masses

Literal

Usage– Politicians try and play the communal card to win elections, since *religion is the opium of the masses.*

Rhyme or reason

Without reason or sense.

Usage– The mentally unstable woman attacked the master without *rhyme or reason*.

Riddled with

Full of.

Usage– The gangster's body was *riddled with* bullets.

Ride a whirlwind

To direct a mighty force.

Usage– The minister is *riding a whirlwind* for putting up a new factory for his sons.

Ride on the shoulders of

To use the power and influence of.

Usage– He *rides on the shoulders of* his brother to get favors from his colleagues.

Riff raff

Vagabond; common masses.

Usage– The *riff-raff* at the fair spoilt my fun.

Right arm

Main support or assistant.

Usage– Deepu was his brother's *right arm*.

Right of entry

Legal right to enter a place.

Usage– The club reserves its *right of entry*.

Ring a bell

To remind you of something.

Usage– The girl's picture *rang a bell* in my brain.

Ring leader

The chief, used in a negative sense.

Usage– Watan is the *ring-leader* of this gang.

Ringside seat

Very close position.

Usage– Tanmay enjoyed the match from the *ringside seat.*

Rise from the ashes

To recover after failure.

Usage– The young star had the good fortune to *rise from the ashes* and achieve success.

Rise from the ranks

To work one's way up from a low position in life.

Usage– The young soldier *rose from the ranks* to become the General.

Rise to the occasion

Prove equal to an emergency.

Usage– The commander *rose to the occasion* and handled the irate mob with dignity.

Rock the boat

Destabilize a situation.

Usage– Dr. Paul was asked by the medical fraternity not to *rock the boat* with his radical ideas.

Rolling in the aisles

When the audience is laughing.

Usage– The stand up comedy act had us *rolling in the aisles.*

Rolling stone gathers no moss

A man wandering from place to place cannot grow roots.

Usage– The army man's son felt quite like the *rolling stone which gathers no moss.*

Roll of Honor

List of those who have died for the country.

Usage– The martyr's mother felt emotional on seeing her son's name in the *Roll of Honor*.

Rome was not built in a day

All things cannot be done instantly.

Usage– Radhika asked her brother to make his project models with more care and patience, saying that *'Rome was not built in a day'*.

Root of the matter

Basis or foundation.

Usage– The investigation committee wanted to get to the *root of the matter*.

Rope in

Bring in, enlist.

Usage– The politician has *roped in* many celebrities to campaign for him.

Rotten egg

A useless person.

Usage– The manager was convinced that Vineesh was a *rotten egg* and would spoil the whole lot.

Rough around the edges

Raw; need polish.

Usage– Garima is a good singer, but a little *rough around the edges.*

Round up
Collect together.
Usage– All the bad characters were *rounded up* by the police.

Rub shoulders
Come into social contact.
Usage– I *rubbed shoulders* with the who's who at the party.

Rub someone the wrong way
To irritate by wrong handling.
Usage– The elders of our family *rubbed young Revathi the wrong way* by nagging her too much.

Ruffle a few feathers
To annoy people.
Usage– Jas realized that he had *ruffled a few feathers* with his fiery speech.

Rule of thumb
Approximate method.
Usage– The *rule of thumb* for converting pounds into kilograms is to divide it by 2.2.

Rule the roost
To be the master.
Usage– Uma *rules the roost* in her house.

Run a mile
To avoid.
Usage– I would willingly *run a mile* than talk to the gossiping old woman.

Run amok
Wild and out of control.
Usage– The crowd *ran amok* when there was the sound of a blast.

Run in the family

To be hereditary character.

Usage– Blue eyes *run in our family.*

Run into debt

To get into debt.

Usage– Aftab *ran into debt* because of his extravagant lifestyle.

Run out

To run short; to terminate; to leak.

Usage– We *ran out* of printing paper.

Run to seed

To go waste.

Usage– His youthful energy is *running to seed* without a proper guide.

Run of the mill

Ordinary and basic

Usage– Though Stupta is an upmarket restaurant, its *run of the mill* décor and food don't live up to its fine reputation.

Run the show

To be successfully managing.

Usage– My brother *runs the show* at all times.

Run your mouth off

Talk too much.

Usage– I don't know how Kukreja handles his clients; he just *runs his mouth off.*

•••

S

Saddle up
To saddle a horse; mount.
Usage– The jockey *saddled up* just before the big race.

Safe and sound
Secure and healthy.
Usage– The little girl arrived *safe and sound* after being involved in an accident.

Safe bet
No risks.
Usage– The investor believed that the blue chip company's shares were a *safe bet.*

Sail close to the wind
To take risks.
Usage– If the leaders do not *sail close to the wind,* how can we expect changes in the society?

Salt of the earth

Decent, dependable, of the highest excellence.

Usage– People like Rabindranath Tagore are *salt of the earth.*

Sands are running out

Time is nearly at an end.

Usage– The fugitive realized that the *sands were running out* for him.

Sap the energy

Exhaust.

Usage– The hot weather *saps the energy* and drains us completely.

Save one's face

Protect one's honor.

Usage– The big company tried to *save face* by giving excuses for the unfortunate accident.

Save the situation

To provide a way out of difficulty.

Usage– He *saved the situation* by agreeing to the terms laid down by the client.

Saving grace

A characteristic which compensates for one's failings.

Usage– The only *saving grace* of the ill tempered star is his generous nature.

Scales fall from your eyes

To suddenly realize the truth.

Usage– The *scales fell from my eyes* when I saw the servant kicking the dog viciously.

School of adversity

Poor circumstances.

Usage– The whole family is passing through the *school of adversity.*

Score off

Achieve a success against; get the better of.

Usage– Pakistan *scored off* a match against New Zealand.

Scot free

To go free; without payment or punishment.

Usage– The juvenile delinquent went *scot-free* after his lawyer pleaded his client's age as grounds for clemency.

Scrape through

Complete a task somehow.

Usage– She barely managed to *scrape through* her exams.

Scream blue murder

To shout loudly in anger.

Usage– She *screamed blue murder* when the waiter dropped hot soup on her dress.

Seal of love

A kiss.

Usage– The priest asked the newly married couple to mark their holy union with the *seal of love.*

Seamy side of things

Sordid affairs.

Usage– The newspapers today focus more on the *seamy side of things.*

Second childhood

Mental weakness in extreme old age.

Usage– Many old people enter *second childhood* after a certain age.

Second nature

A deeply ingrained habit.

Usage– Charity is his *second nature.*

Second thoughts

To reconsider.

Usage– On *second thoughts* she refused to accept his invitation to dinner.

See eye to eye

To agree with.

Usage– Marina and her sister never *see eye to eye* on anything.

See the light

Realize the truth.

Usage– Buddha *saw the light* at Gaya under the Bodhi tree.

See red

Become angry

Usage– When Anuj raised his hand on his wife yet again, I *saw red* and rushed forward to get her out of harm's way.

See someone through

To help in need.

Usage– Amna decided to *see her sister* through her illness.

See through someone
To ignore.
Usage– The doctor *saw through* his ex wife at the party.

Sell out
To dispose entirely of.
Usage– She has *sold out* her interests in this firm.

Send someone packing
To send someone away.
Usage– When I came to know that the servant was dishonest, I *sent him packing.*

Serve one's time
To pass through apprenticeship.
Usage– The young intern had to *serve his time* before he could take up employment anywhere.

Serve time
To undergo a term of imprisonment.
Usage– He is *serving time* for theft and robbery.

Set about
To begin; to take in hand.
Usage– Tambi's master asked him to *set about* his work at once.

Set afoot
To get going.
Usage– The company director has *set the project afoot.*

Set eyes on
See.
Usage– Shreya recognized him as soon as she *set eyes on* him.

Set fire to

Burn.

Usage– The angry mob *set fire* to the house.

Set forth

To start.

Usage– The princes *set forth* on a journey to find the gems.

Set one's heart on

Desire very much.

Usage– Rama has *set her heart on* a new car.

Set one's teeth

Clench the teeth.

Usage– Mohan *set his teeth* when he heard his boss taking credit for his work.

Set out

To begin.

Usage– The young king *set out* on a long journey.

Set up

To erect or establish.

Usage– Pranab *set up* a shop for his son.

Shadow of death

Threatening approach of death.

Usage– The people of Kashmir are tired of living under the *shadow of death*.

Shake the dust off one's feet

To renounce and forget.

Usage– Yashraj *shook the dust of f his feet* after being cheated and decided to move on.

Shape one's course

Direct one's way.

Usage– Vivek knew he had no godfather to hold his hand so he would have to *shape his own course.*

Sharp cookie

Not easily deceived.

Usage– Shambhu is a *sharp cookie* and does not fall for tall stories.

Shed crocodile tears

Pretend sorrow.

Usage– The master said that there was no use *shedding crocodile tears* over something you were not sorry about.

Sheep that have no sepherd

Helpless crowd.

Usage– The unruly mob looked like *sheep that have no shepherd.*

Shell out

Pay.

Usage– He asked her to *shell out* money for the lunch.

Shilly shally

Indecisiveness; hesitation.

Usage– He could not make up his mind and *shilly-shallied* for a while before taking up the new job.

Shoe is on the other foot

Literal.

Usage– When Vikram saw his younger brother as the coach for his team, he realized that the *shoe was on the other foot.*

Shoot from the hip

Talk bluntly.

Usage– The director decided to *shoot from the hip* and not mince words.

Short shrift

Treat rudely.

Usage– The boss gave the new intern *short shrift* when he made a mistake.

Shot in the arm

A stimulus

Usage– The celebrity's endorsement gave the AIDS campaign a *shot in the arm.*

Shot in the dark

Literal.

Usage– It was a *shot in the dark,* but Diva got the right answer.

Show of hands

Vote indicated by showing hands.

Usage– The management decided to take a *show of hands* on the proposed new work timings.

Shut down

Stop working.

Usage– Many factories have *shut down* after the excise duty was increased.

Shut off

Switch off.

Usage– The electricity was *shut off* for a fixed time every day.

Sick and tired

To be unable to tolerate.

Usage– He is *sick and tired* of being at home.

Side by side

Alongside.

Usage– The friends walked *side by side.*

Sight for sore eyes

A most welcome sight.

Usage– The oasis in the midst of the desert was a *sight for sore eyes.*

Sing another song/tune

Change one's stand.

Usage– When the police questioned him about his involvement in the fraud, he started *singing another tune.*

Sit on the fence

Not to take sides.

Usage– Harish *sat on the fence* and watched his friends fight over a trivial issue.

Size up

Take mental measure of.

Usage– The boss *sized up* the new employee before delegating work.

Skeleton in the closet

A hidden family secret, sorrow or shame.

Usage– The news reporter's probe exposed the *skeleton in the minister's closet.*

Skim the cream off

To take the best part.

Usage– She *skimmed the cream* off the whole college for her dance show.

Skin of one's teeth

Escape narrowly.

Usage– He escaped with the *skin of his teeth* during the riots.

Slip of the tongue

Mistake in speaking.

Usage– Manju was careful in her interaction with the director since she knew that a *slip of the tongue* could cost her job.

Snail's pace

Very slowly.

Usage– Things at the legal front move at a *snail's pace* in India.

Smoke and mirrors

Attempt to conceal something.

Usage– The actress' statement was all *smoke and mirrors.*

Snake in the grass

Lurking danger; betrayer.

Usage– The information leak pointed clearly to a *snake in the grass.*

Snap one's head off

To answer irritably and rudely.

Usage– When I asked the young man for directions, he was ready to *snap my head off.*

Someone is walking over my grave

A response to sudden and unexplained shudder

Usage– When the witness shuddered involuntarily while narrating the crime scene, the policeman looked at her enquiringly. "*Someone is walking over my grave,*" she said.

Sound as a pound

Good or reliable.

Usage– Jaldeep's credit rating was as *sound as a pound,* and the bank immediately granted him the loan.

Sour grapes

Jealousy.

Usage– When Sunita criticized her friend for taking up a job in Australia, it was clearly a case of *sour grapes.*

Sow the seeds

To start something.

Usage– Manisha *sowed the seeds* for charity as a way of life in her child's heart.

Spare the rod and spoil the child

Literal.

Usage– Today parents want to be friends with their children and do not believe that you *spare the rod and spoil the child.*

Speak volumes

Literal.

Usage– The deaf and dumb boy's eyes *spoke volumes.*

Spill the beans

To reveal a secret.

Usage– When the police questioned him, Arvind *spilled the beans* about his friend's involvement in the fraud.

Spin a yarn

To tell a story.

Usage– My maid readily *spins a yarn* to borrow money every now and then.

Spirit is willing but the flesh is weak

Literal.

Usage– My mother wants to learn salsa, but cannot; her *spirit is willing but the flesh is weak.*

Spring a leak

Begin to leak.

Usage– The bucket has *sprung a leak.*

Spur of the moment

Without thinking, impulsive.

Usage– He decided to go for his friend's wedding on the *spur of the moment.*

Square meal

A substantial meal.

Usage– The poor boy did not get even one *square meal* a day.

Squeaky wheel gets the grease

The person who protests the loudest get the best service and attention.

Usage– Vanari is a loudmouth and garners the most attention in our office; *the squeaky wheel gets the grease* but is also the first to be replaced.

Stand one's ground

Maintain one's position.

Usage– Despite stiff opposition, Mahiya *stood her ground* on the new policy.

Stars in your eyes

Feeling happy.

Usage– Aastha gets *stars in her eyes* every time she talks about her boyfriend.

Start from scratch

Start at the very beginning.

Usage– When fire razed their factory to the ground, the brothers had to *start from scratch* again.

Steal someone's thunder

Take the credit and praise for something which someone else did.

Usage– Her beautiful younger sister always manages to *steal her thunder.*

Step up

Increase.

Usage– My boss asked me for suggestions to *step up* the production and sales.

Stick out like a sore thumb

To be clearly different.

Usage– The villager *stuck out like a sore thumb* on the college campus.

Sticky fingers

To steal something.

Usage– The new servant worked well, but had to be thrown out because he had *sticky fingers.*

Sticky wicket

In a difficult situation.

Usage– Shirin knew she was batting on *sticky wicket* when the only person who could vouch that she was speaking the truth disappeared without a trace.

Still waters run deep

People who are quiet have hidden depths.

Usage– Her cousin is the strong, silent and mysterious type of man; the kind for whom you say that *still waters run deep.*

Stone's throw

Short distance.

Usage– My friend's house is at a *stone's throw* from mine.

Storm in a teacup

Exaggerate a problem.

Usage– The heated discussion of the ladies was nothing more than a *storm in a teacup.*

Strain one's eyes

Make an effort to see.

Usage– They *strained their eyes* to see who was coming.

Strike a bargain

To come to terms.

Usage– The man *struck a good bargain* with the shopkeeper.

Strike while the iron is hot

To act at an appropriate time.

Usage– The police officer asked the victim's family to ask for damages while the incident was still fresh in the public's mind since it was important to *strike while the iron was hot.*

Stuffed to the gills

Over eating.

Usage– After the lunch, I felt *stuffed to the gills.*

Sum and substance

Gist.

Usage– I asked my friend to tell me the *sum and substance* of the story.

Sweat blood

To make an extraordinary effort.

Usage– My brother promised to *sweat blood* and make it big in the corporate world.

Sweep things under the carpet

To ignore unpleasant things.

Usage– It is better to air your differences rather than *sweep things under the carpet.*

Sweet tooth

Like eating sugary food.

Usage– Rekha has a *sweet tooth.*

Swim against the tide

Face opposition.

Usage– The President of the big company decided to *swim against the tide* and get the proposal passed.

•••

T

Tables are turned
Bring out a complete reversal of circumstances.

Usage– Laila used to play pranks and miss classes as a student. But now the *tables are turned* and she counsels students to be more serious.

Tail between the legs
Like a beaten dog; humbled.

Usage– He left the scene of conflict with his *tail between the legs*.

Tailor makes the man
A man is judged by his clothes.

Usage– She asked her son to dress properly for the interview since there is wisdom in the old adage that *tailor makes the man*.

Take after
Resemble.

Usage– Shekhar *takes after* his grandmother.

Take a leaf out of someone's book
Copy something.

Usage– I have *taken a leaf out of my husband's book* and am always punctual.

Take by the scruff of the neck
Take complete control.

Usage– With rising absenteeism at office becoming a cause for worry, Archna decided to *take it by the scruff of the neck* and deal with it.

Take for granted
Literal.

Usage– When Zahida had a daughter of her own she realized how much she used to *take her mother for granted.*

Take into one's head
To be seized with a notion.

Usage– Sudha has *taken into her head* that she has to study medicine.

Take the bull by its horns
To tackle someone or something directly.

Usage– Vidhi did not want to ignore the servant's habit of pilfering, so she decided to *take the bull by its horns* and confronted him about it.

Take the chair
Preside over.

Usage– Madhu was asked to *take the chair* at the committee meeting.

Take the rough with the smooth
Literal.

Usage– Mother asked Arpit to *take the rough with the smooth* and enjoy his hostel life.

Take your breath away
To be astonished or surprised.

Usage– The mesmerizing performance *took my breath away.*

Talk big

To talk boastfully.

Usage– He *talks big* and annoys his friends.

Talk nineteen to the sozen

Talk a lot.

Usage– Maina *talks nineteen to the dozen.*

Talk out of your hat

Talk rubbish.

Usage– Sarita *talks out of her hat* when she is angry.

Talking to a brick wall

Literal.

Usage– Talking to the reluctant child was like *talking to a brick wall.*

Tall order

Hard to achieve.

Usage– Asking Swarn to finish his work on time was a *tall order.*

Tall story

Untrue.

Usage– Poornima told her mother a *tall story,* but it just got her into more trouble.

Tall talk

Only words and no actions.

Usage– Varun impresses his clients with his *tall talk,* but fails to deliver.

Tarred with the same brush

With the same defects.

Usage– When she was deceived by a jeweler, she *tarred all of them with the same brush* and stopped trusting any jeweler.

Taste of your own medicine
Teach a lesson.
Usage– The old woman got a *taste of her own medicine* when her son refused to go with her to the doctor.

Tear your hair out
Be irritated.
Usage– Don't *tear your hair out* when your children bother you; just take a deep breath and relax.

Teeny weeny
Very small.
Usage– Mother asked her not to step out of the house in her *teenyweeny* black dress.

Teething troubles
Initial troubles.
Usage– The new project had a number of *teething troubles.*

Tell off
Chide.
Usage– The teacher decided to *tell off* the miscreants.

Ten to one
Chances are quite high.
Usage– *Ten to one* it will rain tomorrow.

Test the waters
Experiment to see how successful something will be.
Usage– The big company launched a trial of its new product range in a small market to *test the waters*.

The ball is in your court
It is up to you to take the next step.
Usage– The company has approved your project, now *the ball is in your court*.

The grass is always greener

What others have seems better.

Usage–Our neighbors seem happier than they actually are because *the grass is always greener on the other side of the fence.*

The more the merrier

Literal.

Usage– Raghav wanted to invite his entire class for his birthday party, thinking *the more the merrier.*

The plot thickens

A situation becomes more complicated.

Usage– When Marjorie was proved innocent, *the plot thickened* as the police had to look elsewhere for the real culprit.

Then and there

At the very place and time.

Usage– The thieves were caught *then and there.*

There is never a road without a turning

No situation remains the same.

Usage– When Susan felt disheartened after losing her job, her father told her not to worry since *there's never a road without a turning.*

Thick as thieves

Very close friends.

Usage– Maria and Suraj have been *thick as thieves* since their kindergarten days.

Think aloud

Utter one's thoughts out loud.

Usage– Hamlet was fond of *thinking aloud.*

Thing outside the box
Think in an imaginative and creative way.
Usage– Our teacher always asked us to *think outside the box.*

Third degree
To be put under pressure to tell the truth.
Usage– The terrorist was given the *third degree* at the police headquarters.

Thorn in the flesh
A constant source of irritation.
Usage– Babli's presence was a *thorn in my flesh.*

Thrash a matter
To discuss a subject from all angles.
Usage– We decided to sit together and *thrash the matter* out.

Thrilled to bits
Extremely pleased.
Usage– Kajal was *thrilled to bits* about her new job.

Through and through
Completely.
Usage– He was drenched *through and through.*

Throw a fit
To have a fit; behave wildly.
Usage– When his father refused to buy the new toy, he *threw a fit.*

Throw caution to the winds
Take a great risk.
Usage– Shena threw *caution to the winds* and eloped with her lover.

Throw pearls to the pigs

Give someone what they will not appreciate.

Usage– Giving well meant advice to the rebellious teenager was like *throwing pearls to the pigs.*

Throw the baby out with the bath water

To get rid of useful things with useless ones.

Usage– When Aditi started spring cleaning, her husband asked her to be careful and not *throw the baby out with the bath water.*

Throw your weight around

To make use of one's position.

Usage– The Commander likes to *throw his weight around.*

Thumb your nose at

Reject something.

Usage– The little girl *thumbed her nose* at the dress she did not like.

Tide over difficulty

To surmount problems.

Usage– He was able to *tide over difficulties* by sheer hard work.

Tie the knot

Get married.

Usage– Gerry and Alicia decided to *tie the knot.*

Tight corner

To be in a difficult situation.

Usage– Since I lost that job, I have been in a *tight corner.*

Till you are blue in the face

To say something repeatedly without achieving anything.

Usage– The star denied his affair *till he was blue in the face,* yet no one believed him.

Time of your life
Enjoy yourself.
Usage– We had the *time of our life* at the graduation party.

Tip of the iceberg
That part of the problem which cannot be seen is more serious.
Usage– The sting operation exposed touts selling seats for money in one of the premier medical college, but this was just a *tip of the iceberg*.

Tittle tattle
Gossip.
Usage– Everybody in my school seems to be fond of *tittletattle*.

To and fro
Here and there; coming and going.
Usage– I wanted to know the *to and fro* fare to London.

To a man
Unanimously.
Usage– Everyone present, *to a man,* had tears in their eyes.

To a T
Done perfectly.
Usage– Mohit's arrangement and décor at the party was perfect *to a T*.

To cut a long story short
Literal.
Usage– Interrupting Prashant's account, I asked him *to cut a long story short* and get to the point.

To err is human, to forgive divine
Literal.
Usage– The lawyer appealed for clemency saying that *to err is human, to forgive divine*.

Toe the line
To follow the rules.
Usage– Kedar likes to *toe the line* in school.

Tomorrow is another day
Things might become better.
Usage– When we lost the first match of the series, my father consoled me and said that *tomorrow is another day.*

Tongue in cheek
Not serious.
Usage– I enjoyed Abner's *tongue in cheek* witticisms.

Too good to be true
Literal.
Usage– Usman's good behavior was *too good to be true.*

Toot your own horn
Boast.
Usage– Sridhar likes to *toot his own horn.*

Tooth and nail

With great determination or violence.
Usage– The army was prepared to fight *tooth and nail* in the war.

Touch and go
Uncertain result.
Usage– Promila survived after the accident, but for two days it was *touch and go.*

Tough nut to crack
Literal.
Usage– The crabby old man was a *tough nut to crack* and Sunil did not know how to seek his daughter's hand in marriage.

Tread in the footsteps of
To follow the examples of.

Usage– Let us *tread in the footsteps of* brave and selfless freedom fighters.

Tread on one's heels
Follow close behind.

Usage– The industrialist's son *treads on the heels of* his father.

Turn a blind eye
Ignore.

Usage– Anand found it difficult to *turn a blind eye to* his wife's misbehavior with his mother.

Turn a deaf ear
Ignore.

Usage– He *turned a deaf ear* to whatever his father told him.

Turn a new leaf
Change completely.

Usage– Garima promised to *turn a new leaf* and take her studies more seriously.

Turn one's coat
To change to the opposite side.

Usage– The young political leader was clever enough to *turn his coat* at an opportune time.

Turn turtle
Turn bottom up.

Usage– The car *turned turtle.*

Twinkling of an eye
To happen very quickly.

Usage– The whole incident happened in the *twinkling of an eye.*

•••

U

Ugly situation

In an awkward position.

Usage– The corrupt official's confession put the whole department in an *ugly situation*.

Ugly duckling

An ugly or unpromising child who later develops into a beauty.

Usage– Anjana was the *ugly duckling* of the family who grew up to be a beautiful swan.

Umpteenth time

Unlimited number of times.

Usage– Mother asked him to clean up his room for the *umpteenth time.*

Uncharted water

To be in an unfamiliar situation.

Usage– When it came to investing in shares and stocks Shyama was treading in *uncharted waters.*

Uncle Sam

The United States.

Usage– *Uncle Sam* lures educated Indian young men with tempting job opportunities.

Uncrowned king

Popular hero.

Usage– Ankit was the *uncrowned king* of his class.

Under cloud

Under suspicion.

Usage– The discredited leader was *under cloud.*

Under lock and key

In safe custody.

Usage– Wahida keeps all her cash and ornaments *under lock and key.*

Under someone's heel

To be under someone's complete control.

Usage– David is totally *under his wife's heel.*

Under the radar

Not to be detected or noticed, to be out of circulation.

Usage– Annie dropped *under the radar* after she failed in her class X exams.

Under the table

Bribes or illegal payment.

Usage– Shubh got his loan approved only when money was paid to the concerned officer *under the table.*

Under the mark

Inferior.

Usage– His performance in the boards was *under the mark.*

Under the weather

To feel ill, sad or lack energy.

Usage– She was feeling *under the weather.*

Under your breath

Whisper or say quietly.

Usage– David mumbled an apology *under his breath* when he bumped into a woman.

Under your nose

Something that happens right in front of you.

Usage– The servant and maid were having an affair right *under my nose.*

Under your skin

To annoy you.

Usage– My sister's nagging got *under my skin.*

Unfailing companion

One who accompanies you everywhere.

Usage– A man's dog, money and wife are his *unfailing companions.*

Uneasy lies the head that wears the crown

Literal.

Usage– When I saw the tight security around the industrialist, I thought to myself, *uneasy lies the head that wears the crown.*

Until and unless
Under condition.
Usage– *Until and unless* you come, we will not go.

Up in arms
In readiness to resist.
Usage– Indra is always *up in arms.*

Up for grabs
To be available to the first person.
Usage– The branded clothing was *up for grabs* at the sale.

Up sticks
To leave somewhere.
Usage– Shravan *upped sticks* and went to work in the US.

Up the creek
To be in real trouble.
Usage– When Daman was caught red handed with the drugs, he knew he was *up the creek.*

Up to the eyes
Deeply involved.
Usage– Niara refused to come out and play since she was involved *up to the eyes* in the school project.

Up with the lark
Get up early.
Usage– Shaiffali is *up with the lark* everyday.

Upper crust
Upper social class.
Usage– Yuvi enjoyed mingling with the *upper crust* at the charity function.

Upper hand
To have the advantage.
Usage– Of all the siblings, Kriti has the *upper hand* in Maths.

Upset the apple cart

To throw all plans into confusion.

Usage– These elections may upset the *apple cart* of the ruling party.

Upside down

Topsyturvy.

Usage– The car turned *upside down.*

Ups and downs

Misfortunes.

Usage– He was shattered by the *ups and downs* of his life.

•••

V

Vacant frivolities

Useless enjoyment.

Usage– Father admonished him to stop indulging in *vacant frivolities* if he wanted to rise in life.

Vale of tears

Refers to the world and the suffering it brings.

Usage– Mansi welcomed a new life into this *vale of tears.*

Varnish the story

Make it more interesting.

Usage– Trust little Victoria to *varnish the story.*

Velvet glove

Gentleness concealing strength.

Usage– The king ruled with an iron hand in a *velvet glove.*

Vent your spleen

Express your anger.

Usage– It was distressing to see the weeping woman *vent her spleen.*

Vested interests

Those who have a hidden agenda.

Usage– People with *vested interests* are making a mockery of our democracy.

Vice versa

The other way round.

Usage– My grandfather used to say that either you eat your food or *vice versa.*

Vicious cycle

Literal.

Usage– The doctor told Alicia that her stress led to infertility and vice versa; it had become a *vicious cycle.*

Visible means

Means which are clear to others.

Usage– His wife wanted to stay within the *visible means* of his income to tide over social requirements.

Volte face

Complete change of stance.

Usage– The new president did a *volte face* as soon as he was elected to the post.

•••

W

Waifs and strays

Homeless, destitute people.

Usage– I felt unhappy seeing the *waifs and strays* in the camp.

Wait attendance on

Attend.

Usage– The king wanted his trusted staff to *wait attendance on* the queen.

Wait in the wings

To wait in the background.

Usage– The star's son had been *waiting in the wings* for the perfect role to showcase his talent.

Wake up call

Warning of a threat.

Usage– Junaid's mother told him that his low grades should be a *wake up call.*

Walk a mile in my shoes

Try to understand someone before criticizing them.

Usage– It is easy to advice me not to argue with my son, but if you *walk a mile in my shoes* you will know better.

Walk in the park

Very easy.

Usage– Sidhu behaved as if his new job was a *walk in the park.*

Walk off

Depart; leave.

Usage– He *walked off* from the meeting.

Walk on air

Feel happy.

Usage– When she got admission in the college of her choice, she was *walking on air* for the rest of the day.

Walk on broken glass

To be punished.

Usage– Suraj had Divya *walking on broken glass* when she turned up late for their rendezvous.

Walk out

To leave as a gesture of disapproval.

Usage– The members *walked out* of the Parliament to demonstrate their protest.

Wallflower

A position without power.

Usage– Pratap wanted his wife to be just a *wallflower* and not be involved in active decision making.

War of words

A bitter argument.

Usage– The *war of words* between the couple made the whole scene very ugly.

Warm the cockles of your heart

Make you feel happy.

Usage– The sight of the little girl pacifying her younger brother *warmed the cockles of my heart.*

Warm up

To become animated.

Usage– When I talked of the good old college days, my friend *warmed up.*

Wash one's hands off

To give up altogether.

Usage– I have *washed my hands off* the whole ugly episode.

Wash dirty linen in public

To expose private affairs.

Usage– Let us not *wash our dirty linen in public.*

Watch one's steps

To step with care.

Usage– Govind asked his son to *watch his steps* in college.

Water off a duck's back

To be unaffected.

Usage– Kutty's suggestions were like *water off a duck's back* to his son.

Wear and tear

Loss by way of use.

Usage– Everything undergoes *wear and tear.*

Wear your heart on your sleeve

Show one's emotions publicly.

Usage– Waris *wears his heart on his sleeve* and it is easy to know what he is feeling.

Weight off your shoulders

To relieve oneself of a burden.

Usage– Confessing my mistakes was a *weight off my shoulders.*

Wet blanket

Someone who tries to spoil other people's fun.

Usage– Manjri's mother is a *wet blanket* and doesn't let her go to parties.

What goes around comes around

Literal.

Usage– Anuj always tries to be kind to people around him because he believes that *what goes around comes around.*

What's good for the goose is good for the gander

Literal.

Usage– The salary structure in our company is same for both the sexes, since *what is good for the goose is good for the gander.*

Wheels within wheels

Complicated influences of work.

Usage– There are *wheels within wheels* in the political world.

When in Rome do as the Romans do

Literal.

Usage– When we went to the village we sat on the ground and ate food; after all, *when in Rome do as Romans do.*

Where there's a will a way

Usage– When I saw the poor student stand first in class X boards, I said to myself, '*Where there is a will there is a way.*'

Where there's smoke there's fire

Literal.

Usage– The stars denied their affair as a rumor, but it turned out to be true; *where there's smoke there's fire.*

While the cat's away, the mouse will play

Literal.

Usage– The company staff had a party every day when the boss was out on a tour; *while the cat is away, the mouse will play.*

White as a sheet

To lose color due to shock.

Usage– When the car appeared to be moving without anyone in the driver's seat, Manohar's face turned *white as a sheet.*

White as snow

Pure or uncorrupted.

Usage– The little princess was *white as snow.*

White elephant

An expensive burden.

Usage– Our new manufacturing unit was a *white elephant* since its running cost turned out to be more than we expected.

Whole kit and caboodle

Everything required.

Usage– Avantika promised to get the *whole kit and caboodle* for the trip.

Whole new ball game

Completely new or different.

Usage– Shalabh was a good painter, but becoming a professional artist was a *whole new ball game* for him.

Wide off the mark

Inaccurate.

Usage– The expert's prediction about the share prices was *wide off the mark.*

Wild goose chase

Time spent trying to do something unsuccessfully.

Usage– The police realized that the thief had led them on a *wild goose chase.*

Win by a short head

To win narrowly.

Usage– He was losing the race initially, but later *won by a short head.*

Wipe out

Destroy utterly.

Usage– The whole city has been *wiped out* by the earthquake.

With flying colors

Pass with high marks.

Usage– Nitin passed the exam *with flying colors.*

Within a whisker

Very close.

Usage– Sheela came *within a whisker* of missing the train.

Without so much as a by your leave

Without even asking for permission.

Usage– The new servant left *without so much as a by your leave.*

Woe is me

To be sad.

Usage– Oh! *Woe is me.* I have lost my job.

Wolf in sheep's clothing

Hypocrite.

Usage– Mother asked me not to talk to strangers for one never knows who is a *wolf in sheep's clothing*.

Woman of the world

Woman of fashion.

Usage– Shobha is a *woman of the world*.

Wood for the trees

Cannot grasp the whole because of too much of details.

Usage– I asked Rajat to trim the details from his project because I could not see the *wood for the trees*.

Word of mouth

Orally.

Usage– The new beauty parlor gained popularity by *word of mouth*.

Work like a dog/work your fingers to the bone/work your socks off

Work very hard.

Usage– My driver *works his fingers to the bone* to put his children through college.

World at your feet

When everything is going well.

Usage– The young star has the *world at her feet*.

World is your oyster

To get everything one wants from life.

Usage– When Kanav won the championship he felt that the *world is his oyster* and there was nothing he could not achieve.

Worm himself into anothers's favor

To get into a person's good graces through underhand means.

Usage– He *wormed himself into her favor* to get the job.

Writing on the wall

A happening foreshadowing disaster.

Usage– When Anuradha failed in the pre board exams, her mother asked her to be aware of the *writing on the wall.*

•••

X

X Factor

An unknown factor.

Usage– The dancer lacked that *X factor* which makes all the difference in a performance.

X rated

Not suitable for children.

Usage– The X *rated* movies were kept in a separate box.

XRay scrutiny

Careful examination.

Usage– The whole controversy was submitted to *Xray* scrutiny to arrive at the truth.

Xanthous eye

Prejudice; jaundiced eye.

Usage– I try not to see the world with a *xanthous eye.*

•••

Y

Yawning Gap

Big difference.

Usage– In India, there is a *yawning gap* between the rich and the poor.

Year by year

Yearly.

Usage– India is making progress in business and technology *year by year*.

Yellow press

Newspaper giving sensational news.

Usage– Journalism has now become tainted with *yellow press* everywhere.

Yellow bellied

Cowardly.

Usage– Kshitij was too *yellow bellied* to join the army.

Yes man

Someone who always agrees with people in authority.

Usage– I realized that the director wanted a *yes man* not a secretary.

Yoke of opinion

Force of public opinion.

Usage– The Chief Minister was left with no choice except to accept the *yoke of opinion.*

You are what you eat

Good diet is the key to good health.

Usage– My grandmother always used to say that one should be careful with what goes inside your mouth because *you are what you eat.*

You can catch more flies with honey than with vinegar

Literal.

Usage– The new salesman managed to sell more goods with his sweet tongue and easy smile than the rest of the team; sure, *you can catch more flies with honey than with vinegar.*

You can choose your friends but not your family

Literal.

Usage– Shirin hates her brother and feels that it is unfortunate that *you can choose your friends but not your family.*

You can lead a horse to water but you can't make it drink

Literal.

Usage– Though I'd offered a job to the unemployed brother of my maid, he did not take it up. Well, *you can lead a horse to water but you can't make it drink.*

You can't make a silk purse out of a sow's ear

If something isn't very good to start with, one can't do much to improve it.

Usage– Professor Higgins took up quite a challenge to transform Eliza Dolittle, because *you can't make a silk purse out of a sow's ear.*

You can't make an omelette without breaking eggs

Literal.

Usage– You have to put up with the troubles if you want to avail the benefits of a job. After all, *you can't make an omelette without breaking eggs.*

You could have knocked me down with a feather

Express shock.

Usage– When I heard that Ranjita had eloped with her driver, *you could have knocked me down with a feather.*

You scratch my back and I scratch yours

If you do something for me, I'll return the favor.

Usage– If you don't tell the boss that I bunked office today, I won't tell him that your project was done by someone else; *you scratch my back and I scratch yours.*

You've made your bed, you'll have to lie in it

To face the consequences.

Usage– Aakriti chose science knowing fully well that she would have to work really hard; *she's made her bed now she'll have to lie in it.*

Young for one's years

Bearing age lightly.

Usage–Your mother looks *young for her years.*

Young turk

A young person who is aggressive and progressive.

Usage– Our Parliament has recently seen an influx of *Young Turks.*

•••

Z

Zero hour
Exact time fixed for launch of some program or operation.
Usage– The team had to get together at the *zero hour.*

Zero tolerance
Not to overlook any small or trivial detail.
Usage– Damini has *zero tolerance* for shoddy project work.

Zest and zeal
With fervor.
Usage– Sanjana pursued her studies with *zest and zeal.*

Zigged before you zagged
To do things in the wrong order.
Usage– You should have given in your resignation here only after getting the appointment letter from your new boss; you *zigged before you zagged.*

Zip it
Be quiet.
Usage– The teacher asked the children to *zip it* so she could start the lessons.

•••

Other Books on

WORD POWER SERIES

1. Idiomatic English (How to Write & Speak It) **(New)**
2. School Essays, Letters, Applications, Paragraphs, and Stories For Higher Secondary Students **(New)**
3. Effective English Comprehention Read Fast, Understand Better! **(New)**
4. Latest Essays for College & Competitive Examinations **(New)**
5. Dictionary of New Words **(New)**
6. Art of English Conversation Speak English Fluently **(New)**
7. Teach Yourself English Grammar & Composition **(New)**
8. Common & Uncommon Proverbs **(New)**
9. Effective Editing Help Yourself in Becoming a Good Editor **(New)**
10. Effective English A Boon for Learners **(New)**
11. Essays for Primary Classes
12. Essays for Junior Classes
13. Essays for Senior Classes
14. Dictionary of Synonyms and Antonyms
15. Dictionary of Idioms and Phrases
16. Common Phrases
17. How to Write & Speak Correct English
18. Meaningful Quotes
19. Punctuation Book
20. Top School Essays
21. How to Write Business Letters with CD
22. Everyday Grammar
23. Everyday Conversation
24. Letters for All Occasions
25. School Essays & Letters for Juniors
26. Common Mistakes in English
27. The Power of Writing
28. Learn English in 21 Lessons
29. First English Dictionary
30. Boost Your Spelling Power
31. Self-Help to English Conversation
32. The Art of Effective Communication
33. A Book of Proverbs & Quotations
34. Word Power Made Easy
35. English Grammar Easier Way
36. General English for Competitive Examinations
37. Spoken English
38. School Essays, Letters Writing and Phrases
39. How to Write & Speak Better English
40. Quote Unquote (A Handbook of Famous Quotations)
41. Improve Your Vocabulary
42. Common Errors in English
43. The Art of Effective Letter Writing
44. Synonyms & Antonyms
45. Idioms
46. Business Letters